Praise

'Team coach[...] [...]e intervention
in organisatic [...] [...]e, it is conceptually
opaque, with a [...] [...]iferentiation from its
competitors and [...]ore clarity for those who deliver
it. Gill Graves undertook much more than just
writing a book which makes team coaching practice
more theoretically coherent. This book is properly
evidence-based, providing important insights into
variable and often intangible processes of team
coaching from the perspective of coaches who gave
their time to become not only contributors but
co-researchers. An important read for those who care
about thorough investigation of coaching practice.'

— **Tatiana Bachkirova**, Professor of Coaching
Psychology at Oxford Brookes University

'Gill's work on coaching combines both great
academic rigour and huge practical impact. She has
worked on many high-profile programmes at the
Cambridge Judge Business School, and her work with
managers and leaders at all levels has been inspiring
and transformational. Her work in both individual
and team coaching provides a compelling foundation
for increasing development and performance.
This book is essential reading for people seeking to
enhance their own effectiveness and that of others.'

— **Dr Philip Stiles**, Director of the Centre
for International Human Resource
Management (CIHRM), Judge Business
School, University of Cambridge

TEAM COACHING

WITH IMPACT AT WORK

A Handbook For
Team Coaches

GILL GRAVES

R^ethink

First published in Great Britain in 2024
by Rethink Press (www.rethinkpress.com)

© Copyright Gill Graves

For Mum, Dad and Judith – 'Team Palin',
my family and the ultimate team.

Simply the best!

Contents

Foreword by Dr Paul Lawrence   1

Foreword by Dr Alison Hodge   5

Introduction   9

    Why this book?   13

    Summary of the chapters   15

1 What Is Team Coaching?   19

    Evolving definitions of team coaching   22

    The PiE Team Coaching Model®   27

2 Preparation   37

    Do I need a co-coach?   39

    Do I coach the team leader?   42

    What special care does the team leader need?   46

    Do I coach other team members?   47

    How will I gather insight for the assignment?   50

    How will I structure the assignment?   58

3 Intervention – Support, Challenge And Roles   **61**

Creating optimal conditions for safety
and growth   62

Challenging performance   66

Roles the team coach might play   74

**4 Intervention – What Do Team Coaches
Actually Do In Sessions?**   **91**

Theoretical/philosophical perspectives   93

Personality differences   97

Developmental differences   99

The structure of a 'typical' team coaching
assignment   101

Team coaching tools and techniques   106

Diverse team coaching approaches   111

5 Evaluation   **117**

Evaluating my team coaching work   118

Evaluating the success of team coaching   121

6 Self-care And Supervision   **131**

The importance of self-care   132

Team coaching supervision   137

Supervision and The PiE Team
Coaching Model®   147

Conclusion   151

Appendix A: PiE Team Coaching Model®:
  Supporting Framework   159

    Preparation phase   160
    Intervention phase   168
    Evaluation phase   176

Appendix B: Team Effectiveness
  Survey Example   181

Appendix C: Psychometrics And
  Models Referenced   185

    Books/articles   185
    Resources/tools   187

References   189

Acknowledgements   199

The Author   201

Foreword

by Dr Paul Lawrence

As Gill points out, team coaching is still very much in its infancy. People don't yet agree on what a team is, or what team coaching is, let alone how the aspiring team coach should approach their work.

Traditional definitions of a team emphasise the importance of boundaries, and being clear as to who is on the team and who is not, and they emphasise the importance of stability. But if a team is a group of people working together on a specific issue, then as Mortensen writes, '…boundary change, overlap, and disagreement, however, suggest a different reality, in which teams may be far more fleeting, and 'teams as things' is a less accurate portrayal of the way team members think of them.' These are two quite different ways of thinking about a team, reflecting fundamentally different ways of looking at the world, and there are other ways too of thinking about this idea of 'team'.

How we think about a team inevitably impacts on how we might choose to define team coaching. How we then go about deciding what we will actually do as a team coach, will depend also on multiple other aspects of our world view. In this context Gill's book is refreshing, unlike many other texts on team coaching, in that it doesn't attempt to convince you of the merits of the author's philosophy and preferred approach. Instead, she connects the perspectives of real practising team coaches with some of the literature on team coaching, making explicit some of the key areas of difference in the way team coaching has so far been conceptualised. She *does* offer us a framework through which we can prepare for our work, plan an intervention, and then evaluate our work, while at the same time inviting us to answer for ourselves some of the questions for which there are no definitive answers. These include very practical questions such as:

- Can I work by myself or should I work with a co-coach?

- Is it OK to coach the team leader at the same time as working with the team?

- Is it OK to coach other team members at the same time as working with the team?

As a team coach supervisor, I hear the coaches I work with asking themselves these same questions all the time, often feeling torn between what seems to work best for them and what they are being told they should be doing by writers in the field and other practitioners. Gill makes these questions explicit, within her model, and gives the reader permission to work out the answers to these questions for themselves.

The reader may find the 3Ps framework, as described by Tatiana Bachkirova and Peter Jackson (Bachkirova, 2016, Jackson & Bachkirova, 2019), building on earlier work by David Lane (2006) to be a useful companion piece to Gill's book. The 3Ps model encourages the practitioner to reflect on their own personal philosophy, the theories, models, and frameworks that most resonate for them, and it encourages the practitioner to understand the connection between that philosophy and their own personal life experiences. The 3Ps model also encourages the practitioner to think about their purpose and practice, and how philosophy, purpose and practice all sit together. I find the 3Ps model sits nicely with Ralph Stacey's work on 'practical judgement', the idea that adherence to a generic set of rules, skills or competencies is too simplistic an approach to the work that we do, that we need to discover our own answers through practical experience and ongoing reflection on that practice.

When Clutterbuck et al (2019) say, 'over time, we expect greater clarity to emerge as to what lies in the core of team coaching,' I would suggest first, and most obviously, that such a journey may take a long time, but second, nor should we be particularly concerned as to whether or not we reach the final destination. Gill's findings are based on having spoken in depth to practising team coaches. She describes some of their philosophical differences and some of their, sometimes quite contrary, approaches to their work. We can imagine that all of these coaches have discovered, and are still discovering, ways of working that are helpful to their clients, and I wonder why we would hope for those ways of working to all be similar? We might focus instead, as Gill does, on the importance of supervision in helping people to become ever more aware of the way that they work, and the value of sharing perspectives in service of our collective learning.

As Gill says herself, The PiE Team Coaching Model® is relevant for all team coaches, including the most experienced team coaches. It defines the broad terrain upon which we are all operating, whilst at the same time giving us space to define for ourselves how we choose to navigate that terrain. I commend the book unreservedly for the reflective practitioner seeking to continue to evolve and develop as part of a broad, curious, and ambitious community of people seeking to help teams all over the world to become more effective.

Dr Paul Lawrence, Principal at Leading Systemically and Honorary Research Associate at Oxford Brookes

Foreword

by Dr Alison Hodge

I first met Gill when she engaged me as her supervisor during her training as a coaching supervisor
with the Coaching Supervision Academy (CSA). From
the very start, and what has remained constant, is Gill's
down-to-earth approach both personally and pro-
fessionally. While she has a very strong theoretical
underpinning in her coaching, her supervision and
training practice, she always looks to explore issues
and find solutions that are clear and practical, using
'layperson's' terms wherever possible, uncluttered
with jargon.

Gill has witnessed the changing field of coaching and
now more recently the emerging field practice of team
coaching. As an eternal learner herself, it was an obvious stage in her own development that she engaged

in her doctoral studies to ground her own practice as a team coach and make a positive, evidence-based contribution to the profession. Her blend of practice underpinned by sound theory and knowledge is a hallmark of Gill's professionalism and effectiveness with her clients.

Based on her research inquiry that forms the foundation of this book, she brings the voice of the practitioner into our field in a fresh and enlivening way. She offers case studies with examples from her own and her co-researchers' experience. She has managed to capture both the complexity of the practice, the demands it makes on the coach and at the same time, shares the joy and challenges of this powerful work. This is different from much of the current literature that has emerged in the field so far.

Her book offers a practical resource for team coach practitioners and supervisors. Her lived experience of working with teams for many years has enabled her to capture and share how this practice is far beyond one-to-one interventions in terms of the highs and lows for the team coach. Added to this, as a practising coaching supervisor, she brings clear insights to the relevance and value that supervision provides that allows team coaches to reflect on and explore their team coaching assignments. She explains the importance for team coaches to take care of themselves both during and between team interventions so they can be present and sensitive to what might be happening both to themselves and in their client teams.

I'm confident that Gill's practical, powerful approach to team coaching offered here will expand team coaches and their supervisors' capacity to learn and develop in their own practice. If you can apply this with some of Gill's light touch and bring some of her open and authentic approach to the work, you and your clients will engage with delight in the learning journey of team coaching.

Dr Alison Hodge, Executive Coach and Coaching Supervisor

Introduction

A s a practising one-to-one coach for more than twenty years, I have witnessed the emergence of team coaching and snowballing of interest in it as a distinct form of coaching. The number of organisations seeking it is growing, practising one-to-one coaches are adapting their approaches to meet this emergent demand, and the array of team coaching courses and accreditations is increasing. Commensurate with this rise in interest has been a growth in publications (Clutterbuck, 2007; Thornton, 2010; Hawkins, 2011; Leary-Joyce and Lines, 2017; Clutterbuck, Gannon et al, 2019; Woudstra, 2021) informed by team coaches' own theories and practice.

Despite this increase in interest, a Google search reveals a plethora of definitions for team coaching, including arguments that its primary purpose is developmental, relational, systemic or focusing on performance. In summary, while team coaching is well-established within the world of sport, in the workplace, it is a relatively recent concept, with a distinct lack of consistency in definition and practice.

My first encounter with team coaching was in 2005. I was undertaking a diploma and it was the subject of one of the workshops. Most of the workshop centred on a team-performance model, looking at energy flow and positive and negative behaviours in a team's quest to become high performing. We explored how this model could be used to coach a team using our freshly honed skills and behaviours. I recall being interested, enjoying the session while wondering whether this process was really different to team development or facilitation.

Over the following years, I continued to add to my knowledge of individual coaching, completing my MA in coaching and mentoring and my coaching supervision diploma. I maintained an interest in team coaching, attending the occasional continuous professional development (CPD) session or workshop, as well as working with organisational teams. In hindsight, I did a good job of sitting on the fence while working with teams – straddling two distinct areas by referring to such sessions as 'team coaching and development'.

After one such intervention, I spent some time reflecting on the experience and how a coaching approach now percolated most aspects of my work, including how I worked with teams, contracted with them and provided support and challenge through listening, questioning and using my intuition. Aware that how I was working with teams now was different to how I had worked with them ten years previously, I started to be curious about how my work was evolving and whether this constituted team coaching.

A strong pattern in my professional development has been to underpin my practice with knowledge, which led me to enrol on a team coaching programme. The programme was designed as a blend of team coaching and supervision thereof. The attendees were all professional coaches and supervisors with varying levels of experience and knowledge of team coaching.

What became apparent from the outset was that there was no shared understanding or conceptualisation of team coaching. We explored several models, but while some of the elements of them resonated with us, we all felt that they were too theoretical, too linear and did not capture the messiness of the team coaching that we experienced as practitioners. Even those who had trained as team coaches using a particular methodology were quick to point out that they did not necessarily follow that methodology. I left the programme with more knowledge about team coaching, as well as a number of remaining and new questions.

Over the next couple of years, I continued to explore team coaching through reading and attending workshops, as well as working with teams – now calling these interventions 'team coaching'. At the end of 2016,

I was asked to deliver a session on team coaching at a conference, which forced me to commit my current thinking on the subject into a presentation. The level of energy during the session, number of questions and follow-ups afterwards underscored for me the interest in team coaching, as well as a continuing confusion and lack of understanding as to what exactly it was.

The following year, I decided to take my development to the next level and undertake a professional doctorate. As part of my application for the programme, I had to present my ideas on a research topic. I chose team coaching, inspired by my ongoing quest to make sense of this process as I incorporated it into my professional practice. As a research-practitioner, I was motivated by the opportunity to add to the emergent knowledge on team coaching.

As I honed my research topic into a specific question to study, I became aware that the experience of team coaching was presented through theoretical models by a few leading voices in the field or from the perspective of team members in case studies. What happens between the coach and the team, from the perspective of practising team coaches, was largely absent, and this missing component was important to present a more complete picture of the process.

I formulated a simple research question: what do the experiences of team coaches tell us about the essential elements of team coaching? I deliberately chose the word 'essential' as I wanted to uncover the aspects that were deemed absolutely necessary or indispensable, pertaining to the essence of team coaching. Elements that did not have the same level of importance in other team interventions. Uncovering these essential elements would add to the understanding of both what team coaching is and how these elements are created and experienced by team coaches.

During my study, I worked with practising team coaches, sharing our experiences individually and collectively. The culmination of the study was the development of The PiE Team Coaching Model® and accompanying framework, building upon the findings from the research that team coaching is comprised of three distinct stages: Preparation, Intervention and Evaluation.

Why this book?

Having completed my professional doctorate and published my findings (Graves, 2021), I was met by several people enquiring, 'So, when is the book coming out?' I had independently and concurrently come to the same conclusion: that there was a gap in the market for a team coaching practitioner's handbook, providing an inside account of what it is and how you do it from the perspective of the team coach.

Based on The PiE Team Coaching Model® and accompanying framework, *Team Coaching With Impact At Work* is a resource for practitioners and supervisors. It is also a useful resource for those who are currently engaging in one-to-one coaching to utilise as a bridge into team coaching, enabling reflection on current areas of strength as well as providing additional knowledge and expertise and highlighting areas for development. As such, it provides a practical guide to what team coaching is, how it is different to one-to-one coaching, its demands and what you do when you are team coaching. The PiE Team Coaching Model® and framework are equally useful for those already practising team coaching to further inform and develop their practice, as these resources outline typical practice as a baseline while providing latitude for users to create their own 'brand' of team coaching in line with their theoretical approach.

A key finding of my own immersion into the world of team coaching over the past few years has been a deeper understanding of the demands of team versus one-to-one coaching. The PiE Team Coaching Model® highlights the importance of regular supervision with someone who understands the complexity of working with groups throughout a team coaching assignment, from the start to the finish, with different foci of attention in each phase. This appreciation of the importance of supervision has particular significance for coach supervisors whose focus is currently on one-to-one coaching practice and who may need to review their practice and/or undertake additional CPD to provide effective supervisory support to team coaches.

Throughout the book, I describe essential elements of team coaching, as well as attempting to capture some of the diverse array of differing approaches and practices.

From the outset, the best way of doing so is to use examples from others alongside my own experiences. You will, therefore, find case studies and quotations from practising team coaches. I sought and obtained permission to include these examples and I have used pseudonyms to disguise the identity of the team coaches.

Each chapter is prefaced by a cinquain poem, ie a short poem comprising five lines and nine words, written by a team coach during a focus group I ran when I asked all participants for a piece of prose starting with the words 'My experience of team coaching...' Participants then reflected on their prose, highlighting words which appeared to be particularly significant to them prior to preparing their cinquain poem and sharing this with the rest of the group. I was intrigued and amazed by how it was possible to capture the essence of the joy and challenge of team coaching in just nine words, and when I was thinking about how to transition from chapter to chapter, these poems appeared as the ideal solution. I hope you enjoy them and maybe you will be inspired to write your own.

Summary of the chapters

The chapters are organised with reference to the three distinct phases of team coaching – Preparation, Intervention and Evaluation.

The first chapter, 'What is team coaching? ', explores some of the different conceptualisations and definitions of team coaching prior to introducing The PiE Team Coaching Model® and accompanying framework.

Having introduced and explained The PiE Team Coaching Model®, the book will look at each of the three phases in depth. Chapter Two covers the Preparation phase, Chapters Three and Four the Intervention phase, and Chapter Five the Evaluation phase. The central theme of self-care and supervision, which runs through all three phases, is explored in Chapter Six.

Preparation

Chapter Two focuses on some of the key considerations before embarking on team coaching, from the perspective of the team and the coach. These considerations are:

- Do I need a co-coach?

- Do I coach the team leader?

- What special care does the team leader need?

- Do I coach other team members?

- How will I gather insight for the assignment and from whom?

- How will I structure the assignment?

Intervention

Chapters Three and Four explore the heart of The PiE Team Coaching Model®, the Intervention phase.

Chapter Three focuses on creating the optimal conditions for team coaching, starting with a container of safety and growth (this term will become clear in the Intervention phase) prior to exploring how the coach can challenge the team and provide feedback. The chapter looks at the range of roles that the coach might play during sessions, including roles they have chosen to adopt as well as ones they may be inadvertently pulled into. Chapter Four provides some illustrations of team coaching assignments, including the structure of the assignments and activities taking place.

Evaluation

Chapter Five explores the Evaluation phase of The PiE Team Coaching Model®, including evaluating the success of team coaching, reflective practice, self-care and external support.

Chapter Six examines the demands of supervision and the importance of self-care, as well as charting the role of supervision throughout a coaching assignment, the foci of its attention based on each phase and the particular demands of team coaching versus one-to-one supervision.

The book ends with a summary of current thinking on team coaching, including ongoing debates and areas requiring more knowledge and research.

My experience of team coaching...

Exploration
Action orientated
Effective, inquisitive, questioning
Wider objectives
Space

— Jackie

ONE

What Is Team Coaching?

When choosing a title for this handbook, I deliberately used the term 'team coaching' rather
than 'group coaching' or 'team and group coaching'.
In doing so, I was aware that I was opening myself up
to the question, 'What is the difference between group
and team coaching?' I therefore want to start this chapter with providing my own answer. However, as with
so many questions, the answer is not straightforward.

If we look at coaching literature, we find that it strug-
gles to provide a simple answer to the above question,
with even the most cursory review revealing diverging opinions on team and group coaching. O'Connor
and Cavanagh (2017) summarise the current predica-
ment, 'The literature on group and team coaching is

bedevilled by a foundational lack of clarity' (p 487). They proceed to argue that authors who publish in this area attempt to reduce this lack of clarity by providing specific definitions of what is a team and what is a group, and how this difference has implications for coaching.

I concur with O'Connor and Cavanagh, that the groups versus teams debate is one area that has been covered in some detail in the literature (Katzenbach and Smith, 1993; Hackman and Wageman, 2005; Hawkins, 2011; Peters and Carr, 2013) and more recently in a chapter that I co-authored (Clutterbuck and Graves, 2023). I therefore do not feel a need to add to this debate in this handbook. However, as I decided to use the term 'team coaching' rather than 'team and group coaching', it is worth noting the distinction I am making between the two and how I have reached this position.

Team coaching has historically been described in the literature as engagements with intact teams in which members work together and share responsibilities for the output of the team (Hackman and Wageman, 2005; Thornton, 2010; Hawkins, 2011). By contrast, group coaching is generally regarded as a small number of people who meet together on several occasions for the purpose of learning through exchange and interaction with one another (Thornton, 2010). More recently, this distinction has been challenged as too restrictive as it excludes interventions such as coaching with leaders who all have a shared goal – for example, improving their leadership style – and are seeking opportunities for behaviour coaching in a group (O'Connor and Cavanagh, 2017). Clutterbuck et al (2019) continue this debate by arguing that one of the applications for team coaching is to help a group of people who lack the defining collective characteristics of a team, such as shared purpose and priorities, to become a team.

In my own work, I offer group coaching when individuals from the same or different organisations come together to engage in learning using coaching techniques. Sometimes, particularly if group members work for the same organisation and have similar goals, eg they are on the same leadership programme or have a project to complete together, it is noticeable that the group starts to take on more team characteristics. Examples would be agreeing common outcomes and ground rules for behaviours, and holding each other to account. They may even refer to themselves as a team, I might find myself referring to them as a team, and arguably, the boundary between group and team becomes somewhat blurred.

By contrast, when I am team coaching, I am almost always working with an intact organisational team. Perhaps a team that has just been formed, but more often, one that exists in perpetuity, for example a leadership team. I am invariably invited to do the work because the team has met with some challenging times, has some new members and/or wants to recalibrate and work on how it can be more effective. While being cautious of drawing clear distinctions between groups and teams, I will be using the above working definitions with a focus on organisational teams throughout this handbook.

Evolving definitions of team coaching

The earliest substantive attempt to define team coaching is that of Hackman and Wageman (2005), who outlined an approach that was further developed by Wageman et al (2008). This approach is explicitly non-relational, focusing on where the team is in its developmental journey and designing an intervention accordingly:

> 'A direct interaction with a team intended
> to help members make coordinated and
> task-appropriate use of their collective
> resources in accomplishing the team's work.'
> (Hackman and Wageman, 2005, p 269)

Notably, Wageman et al (2008) advise team coaches not to address personal relationships explicitly, arguing that while such interventions may be enjoyable, they are not likely to lead to improvements in performance.

Clutterbuck (2007) assumes a different stand-point with his definition of team coaching:

'Helping the team improve performance, and the processes by which performance is achieved, through reflection and dialogue.' (Clutterbuck, 2007, p 77)

Here, while agreeing with Hackman and Wageman (2005) that team coaching is about helping, Clutterbuck stresses that this helping goes beyond what the team achieves and encompasses how it goes about this, including the processes. Clutterbuck also refers to the work of Senge (1999), connecting team coaching to organisational learning. Team learning, he argues, is a key ingredient of an organisational learning agenda, and a major focus of team coaching is to help teams, and thereby organisations, to learn and become more effective.

This focus on learning is made more explicit in Clutterbuck's 2014 definition of team coaching:

'A learning intervention designed to increase collective capability and performance of a group or team, through application of the coaching principles of assisted reflection, analysis and motivation for change.' (Clutterbuck, 2014, p 271)

By contrast, Thornton (2010) adopts a psychodynamic approach to team coaching, recognising that the team is made up of individuals who need to collaborate together to achieve performance, with the central role of the coach being to manage relationships.

> 'Team coaching is coaching a team to achieve a common goal, paying attention both to individual performance and to group collaboration and performance.'
> (Thornton, 2010, p 120)

Thornton's approach is, therefore, relational, but also systemic, with Thornton arguing that it is 'at our peril' if we as coaches ignore the system within which our client team operates. However, Thornton advocates caution, arguing that a team coach should only call out the functioning of relationships between team members if this is likely to prove meaningful and relevant to them.

Hawkins' (2014) definition of team coaching has links with both Clutterbuck and Thornton. He similarly advocates that the team coach pay attention to the emotional work of the team and, like Clutterbuck, he regards the team as a learning system. However, while Thornton (2010) promotes a systemic perspective, Hawkins' approach is explicitly systemic, not merely looking at the relationships between team members, but also with other teams.

'Systemic team coaching is a process by which a team coach works with the whole team, both when they are together and when they are apart, in order to help them improve both their collective performance and how they work together, and also how they develop their collective leadership to more effectively engage with all their key stakeholder groups to jointly transform the wider business.' (Hawkins, 2014, p 107)

Hawkins argues that team coaching is a distinct discipline, defining a whole gamut of team interventions including facilitation, development, process consultancy, building and coaching. Equally, he proposes a continuum of team interventions, ranging from facilitation at one end to transformational leadership team coaching at the other.

While there may not be real clarity in terms of what team coaching is and is not, the question remains as to whether the experience of team coaching is substantially different to other group or team interventions. Hawkins (2014) argues that it is, others take a more nuanced approach. Brown and Grant (2010, p 36) believe that there is 'conceptual confusion' as to how team coaching is distinctive from other team-based interventions, arguing that while Hawkins (2014) regards process consultation as a distinct group intervention, Hackman and Wageman (2005) position it explicitly as an approach to team coaching.

Similarly, researchers have expended significant time and effort in drawing a clear distinction between the role of a team facilitator and team coach (Clutterbuck, 2007; Brown and Grant, 2010; Lawrence, 2019). However, attempts to provide clarity between the two are inevitably followed by conclusions that there is some overlap and acknowledgement that the terms facilitation and coaching are used interchangeably in the literature – all serving to blur the boundaries once again.

What emerges is an evolving sense of what team coaching is, with practitioners and thought leaders in the field of coaching conceptualising their own opinion-based practice. This in turn translates into several alternative perspectives about the role and function of team coaching. The common factors, however, include:

- It is a process that takes place over a number of sessions, spread out over a period of time.

- It involves individuals in a team learning together while completing a task/carrying out their business.

- It is holistic, focusing on the whole team.

- It involves work that necessitates the use of a coach (ie it is not simply team building).

- It focuses on the health of the team and long-term change.
(Clutterbuck and Graves, 2023)

As I embarked on my study of team coaching, it was apparent to me that, while the conceptual confusion has been highlighted and explored in terms of definitions, the literature has largely fallen short of describing what is the actual experience of taking part in team coaching, in particular from the perspective of the team coach. A number of models have been developed (Clutterbuck, 2007; Brown and Grant, 2010; Carr and Peters, 2011; Hawkins, 2014) and practitioners have contributed to the team coaching literature by providing case studies (Clutterbuck, 2007; Woodhead, 2011; Carr and Peters, 2011; Dassen, 2015), but there is a paucity of evidence of how these models have been used and experienced in practice, and of the team coaching process: what happens between the coach and the team, the specific coaching activities that take place and how these are similar / different to other team interventions, for example team development and team facilitation. I became particularly interested in this gap in the knowledge of team coaching.

The PiE Team Coaching Model®

At the start of my study, I asked the team coaches I was working with to share their definition / conceptualisation of team coaching, emphasising that I was interested in their current thinking and their own words, rather than those of a thought leader or from any particular model. I share some of these definitions / conceptualisations below.

Helping a team improve its performance and processes through communication, curiosity and dialogue. (Bob)

It's a relationship with a team, where I maintain relationships with individuals in that team to work with them on something important to them to achieve what they want to achieve. (Grace)

Working through a lens, staying true to the ethics of individual coaching. Allowing team members' thoughts to emerge so that they reach the results they're looking for. (Jackie)

It's like a cohesive organism that's made from different parts, where every part understands its role within the greater organism. I know it's a system, but actually, it's also living and breathing and growing like a moving mass. Everyone understands their role within that organism, their own individual roles, and that team coaching enables all of those parts to work together to perform at their optimum while flexing, developing and growing. (Joy)

It's a journey. It's about journeying with people that have a task to do, and navigating the task and how they do it together in the best way in service of the organisation, in service of what they've been brought together to do. Right now, that's what I'm sitting with. How can you get the best results in the best way for the team and the organisation? (Kennedy)

Team coaching is about improving the quality of conversations within the team and with the stakeholders, but it's also about development as human beings and individuals, and as a group, so that development piece shifts a mindset. Emotional intelligence and behaviours are core as well. That's what comes to mind at the moment. (Anita)

The only purpose of a team is to get results, otherwise you don't need a team, so the team in any organisation, any context, is about getting results. The objective, the product of team coaching, is to raise the awareness of the team members, and then equip them in choosing the behaviours that lead to high performance in a sustainable way. When your job's done as a team coach, when they have meetings, they don't ever just attend to the business at hand anymore, but also to the system, every time they meet. There's always two levels of awareness – let's talk about business and what we want to achieve, and by the way, how are we behaving that makes this as much as possible successful, really successful, and ensures we're enjoying ourselves and have a sense of team? (Monica)

It's a bit like the starlings when they're doing their murmuration in the sky. They're all moving in sync with each other and instinctively know which direction they're going in. It's about enabling team members to get really clear about their declaration, what they're committed to, their purpose, and then gain clarity on how they're going to show up and work with each other and embody that purpose in a series of practices. They will come together on a regular basis to do those practices, and by so doing will naturally draw together as a team and create a solid foundation to do what they need to do back in the business, with other people in their teams or stakeholders, having that sense that they've got each other's backs. For me, team coaching is about moving people through this model and getting them to do it in an embodied way so that they are grounded and connected to each other, and they've got a really clear sense of what they are coming together and doing things for. (Jen)

I definitely see team coaching as a journey. It's absolutely the coach and the team in it together for a duration to maximise performance in a sustainable way, totally sustainable. It's not just within the team; it's in the organisation, it's on the outside. It's ensuring they're getting a good understanding, so working on clarity of purpose is really important. Are they doing work only their team can do? While you're coaching a team to be high performing, you are also teaching the individuals. They are learning how to be strong team players wherever they go. (Liza)

An organisation needs to flow towards its intentions, as water always flows to the sea. Sometimes, this flow will be turbulent, sometimes smooth; sometimes it may get blocked. The coach's role with the team is to help them identify its intentions and the state of flow, and to attend to the elements which will create the most sustainable and effective flow possible (not always the fastest). (John)

As everyone shared their definitions, I noticed how many described team coaching as something that takes place over an extended period of time with a sense of movement, direction and change. Some used the analogy of a journey, and while mindful that this analogy is well-worn, I became increasingly aware of how team coaches described the process of team coaching in a number of stages.

They all spoke of a significant number of tasks and questions that need to be considered and answered prior to any team coaching taking place. They described a wide array of activities, behaviours, knowledge tapped into, skills utilised and roles adopted while they were 'in the room' with the team, practising team coaching. Finally, there were insights looking back at past experiences of team coaching, reflecting on their own performance as a team coach (often in contrast to their performance as an individual coach) and how they knew that their interventions had, or had not, been successful, as well as some considerations for team coaching as a growing and emergent practice.

A picture emerged of three stages: a beginning phase; the middle phase, the 'doing'; and a reflection phase. The terms for these three phases quickly slotted into place – Preparation, Intervention and Evaluation.

As I drew the study to a close, I created my own personal synthesis of team coaching, bringing together all of the elements that had emerged into a total experience, showing patterns and relationships. The resultant PiE Team Coaching Model®, shown in the figure, builds upon the findings from the research that team coaching comprises three stages: Preparation, Intervention and Evaluation. Supervision runs throughout an assignment, from the start to the finish, with different foci of attention in each phase.

The left-hand side of the model represents the Preparation phase, with the key questions the coach needs to ask to make informed decisions prior to commencing a team coaching assignment. The questions include how they will gain insight for the assignment and from whom, as well as decisions that will last throughout the assignment: whether the team coach will work with a co-coach; whether they will offer individual coaching alongside team coaching; and establishing supervision support.

At the core of the model is the Intervention phase, where a container of safety and growth is created, complemented by challenge so learning and change can take place. During this phase, the team coach will assume a variety of roles, some by choice and some that they are unconsciously drawn into, and these roles are represented in the model. Finally, the Evaluation phase is the time for the team coach to take stock of the work that they have undertaken on behalf of the client, as well as understanding what they are taking away from this work and bringing the assignment to a clear ending.

The PiE Team Coaching Model® and accompanying framework are different from other team coaching models and frameworks, having been developed through a collaborative research process in conjunction with practising team coaches. They reflect the complexity of team coaching interventions by encapsulating the messiness of the theory in use, and including both universal essential elements and typical variations identified by team coaches.

The model recognises the universal elements of team coaching as well as the fact that there are many divergences in practice. The supporting framework for the model (presented in Appendix A) provides a supplementary resource for the coaching profession, detailing the universal elements as well as typical variations for team coaches to consider in their practice.

The PiE Team Coaching Model®

Evaluation

- How am I evaluating the success of my team coaching?
- How am I taking care of myself? (self-care and external support)
- What patterns/ themes are emerging in my work?
- How am I developing as a team coach?
- How am I engaging in reflective practice? (including with co-coach)

Intervention

- Teacher/Trainer
- Facilitator
- Providing Direction
  - Providing Challenge
- Mentor/Expert
- Referee

Inner rings:
- Being Provocative
- Credibility
- Trust
- Vulnerability
- Observational Feedback
- Psychological Safety
- Transparency
- Safety & Growth
- Holding up the Mirror
- Group Contagion
- Projection and Transference

- Team Member
- Team Leader
- Nurturing Parent
- Critical Parent

Supervision

- Understanding how the work is impacting on the team coach – triggers, projection, countertransference and feelings towards team members
- Emotional space to download and replenish energy
- Standing back and refreshing approach
- Endings
- Stepping out, leaving the team resourced
- Processing any 'hangover' from the work
- Space to reflect on the quality of the work

Preparation

- Do I need a co-coach? If so, who and how and will we work together?
- Do I coach the team leader?
- What special care does the team leader need?
- Do I coach other team members?
- How will I gather insight for the assignment and from whom? (Team members and stakeholders)
- How will I structure the assignment? (Number of sessions, frequency, length. Fluid or planned approach)

- Ethics and boundaries
- Issues of self-deception
- Contracting
- Apprehension about starting the work

My experience of team coaching...

Enjoyable
Supporting, challenge
Difficult, time, contracting
Feedback, trust
Useful

— Kennedy

TWO

Preparation

A s I outlined in the Introduction, my own journey into team coaching was via individual coaching, and this is a route that other team coaches have generally followed. The disciplines of individual and team coaching have some similarities, but they also have some clear differences.

For a practitioner, one of the fundamental differences between the two is that team coaching has distinct Preparation, Intervention and Evaluation phases, with particular importance placed on giving time and attention to the Preparation phase. In my research (Graves, 2021), the Preparation phase was described as having a dual purpose: providing insight for the assignment and opportunity for the team coach to commence creating a safe environment – the latter being essential for the success of a team coaching intervention.

My own research and personal experience support commentary on the increasing awareness of the importance of planning team coaching interventions, with arguments for a 40:60 ratio of preparing for versus running the intervention (Bharuvaney et al, 2019) and a working rule of thumb of there being at least the same amount of time spent in exploratory interviews to understand the team and its context as in delivering the team coaching essentials (Hodge and Clutterbuck, 2019).

Preparing for a team coaching assignment is, therefore, important. The PiE Team Coaching Model® identifies a number of key questions for the team coach to ask and find answers to, prior to embarking on a team coaching assignment. These are:

- Do I need a co-coach? If so, who and how will we work together?

- Do I coach the team leader?

- What special care does the team leader need?

- Do I coach other team members?

- How will I gather insight for the assignment and from whom?

- How will I structure the assignment?

None of these questions have model or correct answers. This chapter will take each question in turn, presenting some of the debates, potential ethical dilemmas and common practices as well as popular variations.

Do I need a co-coach?

Team coaching can be highly demanding of the coach since they need to manage simultaneously the coaching process and the interactions of team members. As a result, many team coaches practise co-coaching, whereby two coaches work with the team, enabling load sharing and the opportunity to provide different styles and a contrast for team members.

For some team coaches, working with a co-coach is central to their practice. The work is proposed and planned based on two coaches, and the only key decision to make is who the team coach might choose to work with.

This approach is typified by Bob:

> 'Another philosophy is, there're two of
> us – 99% of the time there are two coaches
> on the basis that we will provide a range of
> personalities, experiences, insights. In other
> words, four eyes are better than two.'

While Liza outlines a similar philosophy, she introduces an additional nuance of power within the relationship: 'There are two of you and there is always a lead coach.'

This practice brings its own challenges, including managing the dynamic of two team coaches in the room and different relationships at play. Recognising this dynamic, and the potential for it to be unhelpful, John explains how his philosophy is not to co-coach.

> 'For a group of eight, ten, twelve, I've always done it on my own, partly because of the dynamic (of two coaches). Once you start with one-to-ones, who would the team members have the one-to-one with if you've got two team coaches in the room together? Then I'd know half of them, and the other coach would know half of them. It then wouldn't work for me in terms of the way I would like to do the coaching… so the short answer is no, I never have, and as you can see, I would not welcome it particularly.'

Size of team emerges as a key consideration for whether or not to work with a co-coach, with a general consensus that if a team comprises eight or fewer members, the coach may decide to do the work on their own. Above this number, the challenge for the team coach is mentally and physically demanding with so much going on, so many dynamics at play, and they are trying to hold everything in their head with no respite.

While team coaches often cite a preference for working with a co-coach for teams of eight members or more, this does not appear to be a hard and fast rule. Joy volunteered how she would happily work on her own for a shorter intervention:

> 'If the team's under ten, say eight to ten, I'm
> happy to run the team coaching on my own.
> I've done bigger ones, so I know it's hard to
> hold the numbers, there's too much going on.
> I'll do it alone for a one-off, but if it's going to
> be a long intervention, I'll bring two people in.'

Team size is by no means the only factor in the decision to co-coach. Other factors are more pragmatic – in particular, recognition that gaining agreement from the client for two coaches is not always possible, for example if there are budget constraints at the outset. Team coaching is an emerging practice, organisations are still coming to terms with what it is, and as an intervention involving multiple sessions, it is already perceived as expensive. As such, adding in an additional team coach may make the cost seem prohibitive, so a team coach may be reticent about stipulating this as an absolute requirement of them taking on the work. As a result, team coaches sometimes choose to carry out the work on their own.

Nevertheless, it is notable that team coaching in pairs is now recommended by most of the leading team coach training providers, and can be seen as an additional competence. An important benefit here is the opportunity to demonstrate effective learning behaviours and teaming skills to the client team (Clutterbuck and Graves, 2023).

Do I coach the team leader?

While team coaching is a process of a coach working with a team, a number of separate arrangements between the team coach and participants might exist alongside, but outside, the team context. These include individual coaching arrangements as well as the close working relationship fostered with the team leader.

Current practices vary dependent on personal decision criteria, as well as ethical and boundary considerations relating to individual coaching. There are, therefore, no clear and fast rules or best practices. Nonetheless, these are all considerations that the team coach needs to be aware of and form their own decisions on ahead of any team coaching assignments. We will now discuss the range of practices, the rationales for them as well as the various pros and cons.

Opinions on having individual coaching arrangements with the team leader during the course of the team coaching assignment are quite divided, with views ranging from 'it's essential' to 'I never do this', as displayed in the figure.

To coach or not to coach?
Perspectives on coaching the team leader

Team coaches clustered at the 'yes' end of the spectrum in the figure explain their practice as being inextricably linked to the team coaching methodology they have been trained in. For example, one team coach explains her practice as 'the lead coach will coach the chief exec, but it's all very transparent', emphasising that 'people don't worry about it, it doesn't seem that it's on their agenda'. Another dismissed potential ethical considerations, saying 'I have never had a problem. It's not difficult at all for me to respect my contracting with a team, and yet coach the leader as well'.

What is certainly apparent is that, in contrast to the linear models presented in team coaching manuals, in practice, team coaches often experience quite 'messy' starts to assignments due to already being engaged in individual coaching with the team leader prior to being invited to do some work with the team. In such situations, clear contracting and transparency are important. For Joy, this entails sharing the pre-existing coaching arrangement with the team at the outset with the 'agreement that I will coach nobody else'.

Anita's process of managing boundaries is to first contract with the team leader, and then separately with the team:

> 'There's agreement in those contracting
> discussions around what will be covered and
> the structure, how I'm planning to work, what
> questions the participants need to bring in,
> what role they will play.'

An alternative perspective is to adopt the practice of not coaching the leader. John is a proponent of this approach, explaining his decision to never coach the team leader and how he was coaching a team where the leader concurrently had a separate coach:

> 'I'm interested in the whole dynamic between
> the team leader and coaching the team.
> Particularly in relation to Team X, where the
> leader has a coach that's not me. I don't know
> what he talks about with him or her... I don't
> even know who the coach is. What he talks

to me about is the dynamic and the patterns
he's seeing in the team and how we can work
together on that…'

For John, his philosophical position is that there are
too many ethical dilemmas involved in coaching the
leader, a lot more 'Chinese walls' and the challenge of
not allowing things to 'bleed too much'. His practice
is based on previous reflections that some level of con-
tamination could not realistically be avoided and that
as a team coach, he would be changed by that and, as
a consequence, may be less effective.

Consistent with an emergent practice, not all team
coaches have adopted a philosophical position on this
subject yet. Examples would be Grace and Bob, who
describe the question of whether to coach the team
leader or not as something that they are currently
exploring in their own practice, with no immediate
answers. Grace acknowledged that the dilemma 'left
questions for me because I haven't fully addressed
in my own mind what my position is on that'. Bob
referred to how he is 'slowly building it into my practice, just to see if it makes a difference in terms of the
team dynamic if I'm also coaching the leader'. What
is apparent is that team coaches do need to reflect and
come to an opinion on this question prior to it being
raised or finding themselves in an uncomfortable
position with ethical considerations.

What special care does the team leader need?

While team coaches may have different philosophies on coaching the team leader, there appears to be a consensus on the importance of the leader getting preferential treatment, and acknowledgement that they are the most exposed member of the team and their level of vulnerability will be a factor in how open the team will be. Team coaches have described assignments to me that were 'damned' from the outset due to the leader's lack of engagement, as well as providing first-hand explanations of some of the nuanced ways in which the 'readiness' of the team leader might be apparent (or absent), including their ability to be humble, vulnerable, open to feedback, secure in their own role and aware that the team coaching might deliver some unexpected outcomes (Graves, 2021). A further insight is that team leader readiness may be nuanced from 'total buy-in' to 'intellectual buy-in'.

Such insights are helpful for the team coach practitioner, particularly when team coaching interventions are commissioned by those outside the team, for example by human resources. Meeting with and getting the team leader on board at the earliest opportunity is of paramount importance for the ultimate success of the work.

Practically, this preferential treatment typically involves meeting with the team leader prior to a team coaching session, giving them a quick snapshot of any initial diagnostic results before the first debrief so they do not get alarmed or surprised by anything, and having structured high-level conversations with them before meeting with the rest of the team, both to get their impressions and to build trust.

Do I coach other team members?

The question of whether to coach team members, or not, alongside a team coaching assignment met with a similar spectrum of responses as the question regarding the team leader. However, philosophical positions on this question were less fixed.

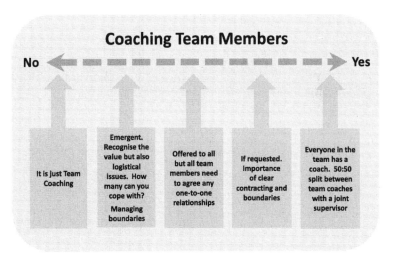

To coach or not to coach? Perspectives on coaching members of the team

The philosophical position on the 'yes' end of the spectrum is exemplified by Liza who described how in her methodology, everybody in the team has a coach, the two coaches split the coachees between them, and the team coaches have a supervisor for the two of them. Having adopted this practice on a number of occasions, Liza described how she believes it works if the contracting is clear and transparent:

> 'A lot is on contracting at the very start because we have to be really transparent on who is working with who, what the boundaries are, what we will share, what we won't share. For example, we won't share anything that goes on in the one-to-one sessions, but if the team members want anything shared, they can tell us or they can share it.'

At the opposite 'no' end of the spectrum, Bob outlined a different philosophical perspective for not coaching team members, having dabbled with it in the past and concluded that it blurs too many lines. '[It] confuses relationships and changes psychological safety in the group.' His current mantra is, 'We're coaching the team and supporting the team leader, but we're not doing anything else.'

As with the previous dilemma of whether or not to coach the team leader, many team coaches appear to have adopted an emergent approach and be currently experimenting with this in their practice. Individual coaching, alongside team coaching, can be particularly valuable when there are themes which are applicable to all team members, or the team needs to make a step change in behaviour which necessitates all members making a change in behaviour, as Grace describes:

> 'There are some conversations you can have in that group context and there are some that are really helpful to have individually in a safer space for the individual to ask, "What's my role in this?"'

However, making a decision to provide individual coaching raises the logistical issue of how many coachees can you cope with? Faced with this dilemma, Grace provided an example of where 'I decided I couldn't possibly coach them all, and I didn't want to have priority relationships with two or three of them, so I chose to coach none of them'. Coaching six or seven team members may feel feasible, whereas a larger team of ten to twelve is too many, resulting in a dilemma for the team coach if they are working on their own.

Faced with potential ethical and logistical issues, Joy described another option, which is to adopt a stance with the desire to be both transparent and ethical:

> '...with a team, we say as part of the pitch "one-to-one coaching is open to you either through me, or through my co-coach, or through anyone else that we think is

appropriate for you, but we will only coach you if the team agrees". The team has to agree that they're happy for us to have that one-to-one relationship, otherwise there's that conflict of interest.'

Overall, the key considerations for team coaches contemplating individual coaching emerge as transparency in who is coaching whom, the importance of contracting and, in particular, that whatever is said or happens in individual conversations stays there and there is no reporting back.

How will I gather insight for the assignment?

As we discussed at the start of the chapter, one of the distinctive features of team coaching, especially when compared with individual coaching, is the amount of time and emphasis placed on preparing for the work. At the core of this preparation is gaining insight from team members and stakeholders to inform the work prior to designing the team coaching assignment.

Gaining insight from team members and stakeholders before embarking on a team coaching assignment is something team coaches agree on, although how they gather this insight and the degree to which they insist upon it varies. Although not necessarily recognising gaining insight as a 'red line', without which they would not engage in a piece of work, some team coaches describe an approach that appears non-negotiable.

Reflecting on his own practice, John muses:

'I probably don't have any real red lines, but I would say that's the way I like to do team coaching, therefore this is what it will all cost. That's what I'm contracting for and if you decide not to do it, let's talk it through. Let me tell you the virtue of this preparation... With team coaching, I don't think I've ever not done it that way, because it helps me to feel comfortable... so yes, I say yes, it's a red line!'

Having one-to-one meetings with stakeholders serves a number of purposes, with different aspects being more or less important for different team coaches. An obvious benefit is that they are useful for picking up themes and trends in the organisation, and key issues facing the team, and to ensure that these are heard from all team members and not just from a selected few.

'The stakeholder interaction that you have at the beginning is never the whole story, and so it's easy to get wrong-footed in the first session about where people are coming from.' (Grace)

'In systemic terms, it's everybody's individual truth. What is it really like to be a member of this team? What's your truth as you sit in this team, as you work in this team?' (Kennedy)

The practice of having one-to-one sessions is reinforced by challenging previous experiences. An example would be Jen, recalling a particularly painful team coaching intervention when she had not had one-to-one meetings with the participants in advance and only had insight provided by the team leader:

'One of the things that I found difficult was not having that one-to-one relationship. I'd stand next to somebody at the coffee station and have a conversation, but that was all I'd have with them, so I didn't really know them that well. That knocked my confidence.'

One-to-one sessions undoubtedly have multi-faceted benefits. For Joy, they serve as an opportunity for team members to have a cathartic 'bitch and moan'.

'For me, this is a parking lot. This is your bitch and moan session. You can raise it [this issue] again, but you can't moan about it!'

This cathartic session has a dual purpose. The team coach hears the unblemished 'truth' while starting the trust-building process with individual team members. What is said in confidence remains confidential with only themes shared back. As Joy says:

'For me, the moans never go anywhere. The themes are the only things that come out, but the team members sit and inform us, and that's why nothing comes out of left field that we haven't heard about before, because they have felt totally safe to say it.'

In the second phase of team coaching, Intervention, we start off by emphasising the importance of building a safe container, a relationship of trust, for the coaching work to be done. What is apparent is that this trust-building work starts much earlier during one-to-ones, a process summarised by Grace:

'This whole idea of enrolling individuals into the coaching process and building the trust with them, it's quite hard to do in a room with people you've not met before. You don't know what the nuances are… The relationship that you have with the team and the permission for them to trust you to take more risks, perhaps more quickly, comes from those initial conversations and relationship building to show why you're there.'

While team coaches emphasise their preference, or in some cases requirement, to have one-to-ones with team members, the form of these varies significantly. Practices range from asking a number of standard open-ended questions to all team members, to the use of a team diagnostic to gain insight against a range of factors, with the output fed back to the team at the first session.

Factors affecting the data-gathering process used include the team members themselves, the budget and what needs to happen. In situations lacking the budget and/or appetite to use an accredited team diagnostic, team coaches will often use a team-effectiveness questionnaire that they have pulled together themselves based on various sources. An example would be Appendix B, a questionnaire that I have used myself, which includes a number of questions with a rating scale as well as open-ended questions for team members to respond to.

If there is sufficient budget and a sense of needing some kind of model to help the participants appreciate what a good team looks like, a bespoke team diagnostics survey can be helpful to gather data, and then present how the team performs against various conditions. There are a number of team diagnostic instruments available, with probably the most common being The Team Diagnostic Survey (TDS); TCI Team Diagnostic™; Team Accelerator Model; the Hogan Team Report; the Rocket Model™; and Strengthscope. Details of all of these, and other tools referenced in this handbook, can be found in Appendix C.

Some team coaches take insight gathering to another level, advocating extending this to encompass key stakeholders, including the team's commissioner (team's boss) and internal and external customers, using varying methods of gathering data. Liza extols the benefits

of using a standard questionnaire with team members
and stakeholders:

> 'There is often a mismatch between how the
> team members see themselves and how the
> stakeholders see them and even how their boss
> sees them. I find this very risky. The beauty
> is if you are using one of these diagnostic
> questionnaires, it covers this, so it's quick and
> easy to get insights and see the differences.'

Insight gathering can also take the form of stakeholder
interviews or focus groups, with the same questions
discussed with all groups or a set of questions, developed by the team coach, sent to various stakeholders.
Faced with budget constraints, dislike of formal diagnostics or other pushbacks, I have used these five
questions to get insight from stakeholders:

- What are your expectations of this team?

- How well are they performing against
  these expectations?

- What is your experience of this team, positive
  and negative?

- Is there anything that this team is not doing that
  you want them to do?

- Is there anything else that you want this team
  to know?

Gathering information is important, can take various formats and includes different degrees of thoroughness. Three different approaches adopted by three experienced team coaches are provided below.

GAINING INFORMATION PRIOR TO A TEAM COACHING ASSIGNMENT IN ACTION

Anita's approach:

'I meet with the leader first to agree objectives, talk about the process and what they want to get out of it. I then go through the same process with the management team. I always recommend that we do stakeholder interviews to get that perspective as well.

'I would then do interviews with the management team. If I can, my preference is to do the TDS, but if this is not possible, I put together a small number of questions, based on the team, to ask everyone. I conduct the interviews, collate the information, bring it back to the management team and go through it with them, encouraging them to pull out the key themes emerging. I get team members involved in analysing the data, so they engage with the data to form their own pictures and ultimately decide what we are going to do, the plan. Then we contract the next steps.'

Bob's approach:

'There is a sense of needing some kind of model to help the team know what a good team looks like. I use a team diagnostics survey, eg the Rocket Model, and that just sits in the background for us to go "Here's what a high-performing team has as components, let's benchmark our conversations". We can then do a bit of mapping and data collecting.

'I always look to provoke an awareness of how members perceive the team and include the stakeholders to get the outside-in view of the team as well as what the members think of themselves. When I feel I need something more robust and research-based, I will use the TDS. I tend to use one of these two.

'For me, the importance of the model is that it is a model of team performance as opposed to one of personality. It is a holistic model that looks at team performance, task and team work.'

John's approach:

'I would normally want to enter into a team coaching assignment by contracting with the team leader and working out what we're trying to achieve. There is an element in team coaching where you have particular responsibilities to the person who is leading that team, because their agenda for the team will feed into your agenda – so they're always going to be close together.

'After contracting with the team leader, I would normally hope to be able to meet every member of the team for the best part of a couple of hours to do Myers-Briggs Type Indicator® (MBTI) or similar to understand what their perspective on the team is, what they think is going well at the moment, what their sticking points are, where the developments might need to be. I would then bring the team together for a day where we would look at some of the implications of their responses and do some of the trust-building stuff, and then start from there.'

How will I structure the assignment?

The final part of the Preparation stage is to design a team coaching assignment. While there is much agreement among team coaches and training providers around gaining insight prior to team coaching assignments, practices are noticeably divergent regarding the design of the assignment itself.

The table below summarises some of the approaches adopted, indicating those that can be regarded as typical as they have been mentioned by several team coaches/training providers, as well as any notable variations. As you can see, practices polarise around the length of assignments and regularity of team coaching sessions, while there is some convergence in terms of the number of sessions, size of the team and length of the sessions.

Having answered the questions outlined at the start of this chapter, gathered insight from team members/stakeholders, and then designed and agreed the scope of the team coaching intervention, the team coach moves their attention on to the intervention itself. The next chapter explores how the team coach sets about creating a safe space, a container, for the work to take place and describes the roles they may find themselves playing during the course of the intervention.

Planning the team coaching intervention	'Typical' approaches	Variations
Length of assignment	No consistent approach. Contracting tends to be about the number of sessions rather than the length of the assignment	No fixed timescale. Work with the team as long as is productive. Contract for a defined period of time, eg one year; four to six meetings this year, and then review
		Assignments are twelve to eighteen months
		Assignments are six to nine months
Size of team	Five to twelve. Eight usually maximum size for working on your own. Up to twelve with a co-team co-coach	
Number of sessions	Typically four to six sessions	With longer assignments, can be up to twelve sessions
Regularity of sessions	No consistent approach	Spacing of sessions varies from monthly to every two months, quarterly or twice yearly
		With dispersed teams, some meetings may be via phone or video in between face-to-face sessions
Length of sessions	Typically half-day sessions	One full-day 'kick off' followed by shorter half-day sessions
	May start with lunch for ice breaking, followed by session of around three-and-a-half hours	One to two days of 'kick off', then at least one half- to one-day follow-up three months later
		Full-day sessions. Morning is a normal team meeting with team coach observing or facilitating. Afternoon is team coaching

Table 1. Planning the team coaching intervention

My experience of team coaching...

Oil
Machine works
Grit makes pearls
Stronger parts
Ready

— Liza

THREE

Intervention – Support, Challenge And Roles

At the core of The PiE Team Coaching Model® is the Intervention phase where a container of safety and growth is created, complemented by challenge, for learning and change to take place. During this phase, the team coach will assume a variety of roles, some by choice and some that they are unconsciously drawn into.

The Intervention stage of the model, showing these roles, is illustrated in the image below.

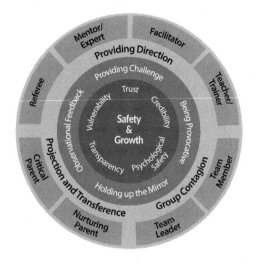

*The Intervention phase: Roles coaches adopt or
are unconsciously drawn into*

This chapter will explore the various ways in which team coaches create a safe space and an optimal level of challenge prior to looking at the range of roles that they may find themselves adopting during an assignment.

Creating optimal conditions
for safety and growth

A safe space, created between the team coach, leader and members, is one of the foundational pieces of team coaching. This idea of a safe space is covered extensively in the coaching and team literature, in particular the concepts of 'psychological safety' (Edmondson, 1999) and 'holding' (Thornton, 2010), and creating a 'container' for the work (Lawrence, 2019).

In speaking about their work, team coaches provide a strong insight into some of the various ways in which they go about establishing this safe space. Anita emphasises the importance of psychological safety and team members 'getting to know me as much as they need to':

> 'I give them a bit about me, my background, how I work. I explain the process, how it works, the boundaries, confidentiality. There's something about how I show up. I show up grounded, confident. I take time before I go in to see a team to be mindful of myself and make sure I'm in my body, which is important, not scatty in my head or all over the place.'

Perhaps unsurprisingly, team coaches describe how they use coaching behaviours, skills and knowledge, honed from years of practising individual coaching, to create a safe team space. Bob identifies:

> '…the ability to ask good questions, to pay attention, to be able to explore below the surface, not just what's being said. The ability to be curious and inspire curiosity in the team. Respect of the individual, being sure you hear their voices, bringing in other voices.'

Grace emphasises listening as 'probably the most important thing… listening with my head, my heart, my ears, my eyes, the whole thing'. A slightly different perspective on using coaching skills is provided by Kennedy when describing how she uses her knowledge of transactional analysis (TA) as a framework for creating a safe space, modelling 'adult' while encouraging a different, creative 'free child' space:

> 'I hold as much of a neutral space as possible, a safe space, trusting them, trusting the process, being that adult in TA, their window on the world: "I'm OK, you're OK." Sometimes, free child turns up, being creative: "OK, let's try something different!" It might be by offering a constellation or a map, or moving around – "Let's play musical chairs, let's see how sitting somewhere else is going to change things. Let's just try it out!" – that the creative free child, the free spirit turns up.'

Creating a safe space is, therefore, something that team coaches work hard on at the outset, as well as it remaining a constant work in progress throughout an assignment. The ability to role model behaviours for a team is both an important and a common practice for team coaches, including individual and teaming behaviours when they are working with a co-coach, but there are divergent approaches in what my co-researchers choose to role model.

Anita and Bob both describe how they deliberately use humour. Anita jokes about herself and role models 'vulnerability, to a degree', and Bob uses it as a 'way of [the team members] making contact with me; of showing that it's not life and death'. Monica describes how she role models confusion or vulnerability in a deliberate attempt to normalise these feelings:

> 'I will say, "I don't know" or "I'm confused right now" or "I'm puzzled", showing them [the team members] how it's possible to be confident, and yet not know and have to ask the question and to say how you feel on occasions.'

Closely aligned to psychological safety is the importance of building trust. As described in the previous chapter, meeting with team members individually in the Preparation phase is regarded as an invaluable means of gathering information on them and the team. In addition, these sessions serve as an opportunity to start building trust with them. Joy's words typify this sentiment:

> 'The initial conversation stage, that initial diagnostic, is really useful because it sort of does that trust build between us. Because the team members know at that stage what they've told us, and they never usually hear it come back out again, so they recognise that they can have that conversation.'

Bob extends this theme by reflecting on the importance of how he presents himself in the first team coaching session, mindful that this session creates the space for the remainder of the work:

'I need to demonstrate in the first session together that I'm a safe pair of hands for them [the team members]. That I'm managing the process confidently gives them a sense of freedom – if the coach isn't going to be fazed by what you're saying, then you're much more likely to say what you think, aren't you? That's the sort of space I try to create with a team – the one where, because it's not going to throw me, it's not throwing them. As safe a space as I can, I guess.'

The ability to create and nurture a safe space emerges as an essential element of team coaching, something that it is vital not only to introduce at the outset, but also to sustain and develop throughout the assignment.

Challenging performance

Once, and only once, they have established a safe space, team coaches will then think about how they challenge team members around individual and collective behaviours to focus on maximising the performance and development of the team. Thornton (2010) provides a helpful framing for what she calls 'holding' (support) and 'exchange' (challenge) and how the two are inextricably linked. Without the former, team members will not feel safe enough and there will be insufficient trust. Without the latter, the climate is too supportive for any meaningful change to take place. This relationship between support and challenge is represented in the illustration at the start of the chapter, with the second circle encasing the safety and growth circle identifying some of the various forms challenge can take, from high challenge and provocative interventions to less direct approaches.

An example of the more provocative and direct approach to challenge comes from Joy, who describes how she can be 'quite direct', once the team has got used to her, and being comfortable calling out behaviour. She recalls:

> 'We got to one bit and the leader said, "Oh, we just haven't had time. We've got to get involved with things – we've got a whole challenge with our clients, who require us to get involved." I said, "No, sorry, that's bullshit. I don't buy that at all. Why have you got to get involved? You're a senior manager, you've got loads of people underneath you. Why?"'

Team coaches often describe challenge in terms of a spectrum of approaches that they adopt. For Bob, his spectrum ranges from 'calling out or being curious about the dynamics' to the 'bigger challenge of "we're getting nowhere here"'. Musing on the subject, he acknowledges that he could be evoking or provoking challenge:

> 'My default is more of an evoker of challenge as opposed to being too "Gordon Ramsay" about it. I will be thoughtful about the challenge and having a co-coach makes me better at that.'

While still using the term 'challenging', other team coaches describe a style that is less provocative and direct, and only used in particular circumstances. An example would be John, who reflects on how he is comfortable challenging, but that there needs to be a real reason for this:

> 'I will be quite challenging, probably around the values… stuff that doesn't fit with what the team has told me. I will sometimes step in and say, "Well, how does that fit with this? There's a whole lot of stuff about integrity here [in the company values]. How would some members of your staff hear the conversation that we've just had?" I'm fairly comfortable doing that kind of thing.'

This kind of challenge is often referred to in the form of a metaphor or analogy, the most commonly used analogy being holding up the mirror. This is a technique of holding the space and inviting team members to look closely at themselves and their actions.

The balance between support and challenge is equally important in individual coaching. In *Challenging Coaching*, Blakey and Day (2012) explore the journey from support to challenge and identify the optimal space of high support/high challenge, which they label 'loving boot high performance'. However, in team coaching, there is the additional tension of how and when to challenge in a team setting. I have certainly been aware of some of the tensions I have experienced around challenging individuals in a group or team setting, with one such reflection captured in the action example below.

CHALLENGE IN ACTION - EXTRACTS FROM MY REFLECTIVE DIARY

For my second coaching session with Team X, a dispersed team using Zoom, I went into it feeling positive. The first session had been brilliant, the team had really gelled.

One person, Mary, hadn't been able to make the first session and had sent her apologies. I was really knocked off my stride right at the start of the second session when Mary smiled. It felt like a disingenuous smile, and she then cut in and asked me the purpose of the sessions, stating that she would never have a meeting without first agreeing an agenda.

'I'm just being transparent,' she said. 'I'm actually amused.'

For some reason, the word 'amused' really jarred with me. I felt judged, defensive. I wanted to challenge her as I would in an individual coaching session, but I held back – it was her first session; challenge felt too early for this team, whose members all seemed to be in high avoidance mode, drinking coffees, looking away, etc. I held back where the individual coach version of me would have given some observational feedback at this point in time – what I was seeing and feeling.

After the call finished, I reflected on what had bothered me so much about this session. There were a number of aspects:

- Being challenged in front of the others, I felt my credibility (which I'd worked so hard on in the first session) was at stake.
- No one else had spoken out.
- It felt like I was being tested.
- There were several levels of dialogue going on.
- I wanted to call Mary out, but felt it was too soon.
- Her smile confused me.
- I wasn't sure where the conversation was going.
- I'd been complacent, expecting my 'lovely team' from last time, and hadn't taken into account that Mary hadn't been there.
- I was aware that I'd been smiling on the outside, but inside, lots of different conversations were going on.
- I was aware of the impact of one negative person and how this affected me.

If this had been individual coaching, I would have felt more resourced to address Mary's behaviour there and then, but the challenge of the team setting, it only being the second session and the first for Mary, and the fact that we were on Zoom all made me hold back. Could I have done a better job? Should I reach out to her separately? Unsure, I decided to take this to my supervisor next week.

In the fourth coaching session with Team X, Mary said she felt relaxed and shared her experience of using my 'How are we showing up?' check in at the start of what she'd anticipated would be a difficult meeting with her boss. She told how her boss had replied, saying, 'Not great, I've just been to a friend's funeral', which took the conversation to a different level. She went on to describe how she was using this check in at all of her meetings and experimenting with having a more emergent agenda.

While Mary didn't say 'Sorry' or 'I was wrong', the sharing of her experiences felt even more powerful than if she had. She showed her vulnerable side. I noticed how the rest of the group smiled broadly at the end of her check in – there was a palpable 'respect Mary' feeling!

My learning, having processed both of these experiences at supervision, was that sometimes it is best to just hang on in there. Building trust takes time. While not challenging Mary had felt uncomfortable at the time – I felt as if I was sitting on my hands and was comparing what I would be doing now in individual coaching with how I was behaving in a team setting – it had been the right move in hindsight. If I had challenged her earlier, perhaps I would have lost Mary and there was a danger that the rest of the group would have sided with her.

It was also a useful reminder that the group you say goodbye to in one session is not the same group that you say hello to in the next. Much has happened in the intervening period and, as coaches, we need to be ready for what presents itself on that day.

My discussions with fellow team coaches reassure me that others experience similar challenges. Kennedy speaks about the difficulty of 'challenging or pressing pause or time out' as she knows team members as a team, but not individually. For Kennedy, the dynamic about when and how to challenge is 'much more present' in individual coaching where 'I know it and I sense it', versus 'five people and what's going on for them that day, that month, when they come into the group'.

Liza acknowledged her comfort level in challenging in an individual versus a group setting.

> 'I find it much easier to do with an individual
> in a one-to-one than in front of the group.
> I know we've contracted that it's OK to call it
> out and name an individual, but if it's one-on-
> one, I can say, "Jane, what are you doing right
> now?" Whereas in a group, I sometimes think,
> "Aw, is it fair to call it out now?"'

Team coaches often describe the skills and behaviours they draw upon to present challenge, citing examples. Monica describes how she might sit in on regular team meetings, observing, and then pressing the pause button and asking, 'What are you noticing right now? What is happening for you now? What do you think is happening in the room, or what isn't being said?' Grace outlines a slightly different approach where she might make her own observations, perhaps referring back to the contract and offering some helpful tips, often early on in the process as a way of getting the team to develop ways of operating that she can also refer back to.

The 'do I raise this now or not?' question is a recurring dilemma with team coaches using similar criteria to make a decision, including hearing a story that seems to be repeating itself and noticing a pattern that keeps coming up or going round in circles. A typical example is provided by Kennedy:

> 'I observe something, maybe I notice a pattern, and at some point in time, I call it out. It keeps going round in circles, keeps coming up. If it happens once – if it's something I've noticed and wondered if it'll happen again – I just hold it in my awareness. If I see it as a pattern going round in circles, then I flag it up.'

The team coach's philosophical grounding appears to be intertwined with their approach to challenging the team and, in particular, how they present challenge. For example, Gestalt practitioners Anita and Bob describe how the use of self is a key technique for them, recognising how something is impacting on them and verbalising it with others. (See Maxwell and Bluckert, 2023, for an evaluation of how the Gestalt theoretical perspective influences the coaching approach.) Anita speaks about 'bringing it into the here and now and raising awareness on how what the team members are experiencing is impacting on them and others'.

Like Grace and Kennedy, Anita and Bob state that the decision to share what they are noticing with the rest of the team is one they wrestle with. For Bob, when he does decide to share – for example, 'I'm bored right now, is anybody else feeling this?' – he recognises that this requires some bravery on his part.

While there are some notable differences in team coaches' perceptions of what constitutes challenge and how they themselves challenge in a team setting, there is general agreement that challenge and time are related, with the former increasing as familiarity with team members increases, as depicted in the illustration below:

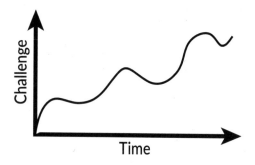

A representation of the typical relationship between time and level of challenge

Roles the team coach might play

While much emphasis has historically been placed on attempting to define team coaching as a distinct discipline to be adopted in preference to facilitation, consultation or training (Clutterbuck, 2007; Grant, 2009; Hawkins, 2014), there is growing recognition that skilled and trained coaches will likely employ a mix of coaching, facilitation, consultation, education and training skills to effectively support the team (Peters, 2019; Lawrence, 2019). Thornton (2019a) draws attention to 'who or what am I invited to be?', referring to the roles the coach may unwittingly be drawn into, as well as the importance of countertransference – 'what feelings do you have in the room/are you left with afterwards?' (p 216).

The range of roles that the team coach might choose to adopt, as well as the ones that they may be drawn into, are described below.

Providing direction: Roles adopted

While recognising that they attempt to spend most of their time in the coach role, team coaches describe other roles that they deliberately adopt on occasion, especially those that involve providing some input and direction for the team. In my own research (Graves, 2021), the roles of mentor/expert; teacher/trainer; facilitator; and referee emerged as those team coaches felt they had some legitimacy in team coaching.

These roles were discussed in focus groups and, while there were some diverging views on how much a given role should be present in team coaching, there was convergence on the descriptions of each role when it was performed appropriately, as well as what was happening when the role was overplayed. These descriptions are summarised in the table below:

What roles might I choose to adopt? Why, how and when?	 Performed well	Overplayed
The mentor or expert	• The coach brings in outside knowledge, eg of industry trends or the wider strategic perspective for the team to accept, reject or keep. They share their knowledge to provide insight/perspective.	• The coach is talking too much, sharing too much of their own expertise with the team, giving their opinion. It's more about the coach than about the team. • A role that can be projected on to the team coach by the team.
The teacher or trainer	• The team coach transfers a lot of what they do as skills to the team, sometimes through demonstrating the process (eg listening, asking questions, observational feedback) and sometimes through explaining, eg sharing a model to explain what might be going on in the team.	• The coach is doing too much of the talking, oversharing of models or theory. • They are feeling the pressure to 'give value for money.

The facilitator	• The coach is facilitating the process, designing the day, the flow of the session, the room, seating; creating and holding some structure and the time.	• The coach is grabbing the markers and flip-charting the discussions, starting to drive the agenda, pumping their energy into the room, being too active, filling silences. • They are feeling uncomfortable, diverting attention elsewhere.
The referee	• The coach is managing the process, helping the team make proactive, deliberate choices about what they're doing in the moment rather than being so free-flowing that it just flows away. Pointing out when 'we're off the pitch', eg not living out values, or going off topic.	• If overplayed, the referee can become the marshal, being too directive with the team.

Table 2. Providing direction – roles adopted by the team coach

Roles the team coach may be drawn into

One inherent risk of working with a team for a lengthy period of time is group contagion, with the team coach gradually losing a sense of distance and objectivity, and effectively turning into a team member. An example of this is provided by John, who describes how familiarity can lead to a lack of rigour on the part of the team coach, resulting in them forgiving or ignoring behaviour that they would previously have challenged:

> 'The danger is that, the longer you work with the team, the more you are likely to become part of it and not address things that you should address because it's "just the banter" or "ah, we've come across that before", and you let it go because you let it go last time.'

While team coaches might recognise group contagion as a potential issue, they express how they start to realise that they are becoming part of the team in different ways. For John, it is the transition from being the referee at the start of the assignment to 'playing with the ball rather than standing back and looking at the interaction of other people playing with the ball'. 'Playing with the ball' means becoming a team member in group discussions, stepping in with solutions or opinions too readily.

Liza experiences a different aspect of group contagion as a sense of losing objectivity. Team members start to 'hit buttons' for her, which could result in her taking sides in the team.

> 'I'm thinking, "If you don't shut up in a minute… no wonder people don't want to come and talk to you because you take up so much time and we don't get anywhere!" It's when you stay objective that you get so much feedback about people. I get sucked into things like that and I really do have to manage myself.'

Another aspect of group contagion is the danger of starting to 'collude' with team members. This danger appears to be more prevalent with team coaches who describe their coaching style as strongly empathic with self-knowledge that they could at times be overly supportive of their coachees. As someone who recognises this pattern in herself, Liza shares the dangers of being sucked into being overly supportive of the team – 'It really is tough for you guys' – or of responding to the invitation 'What do you think we should do?' resulting in her becoming a decision maker.

The role of 'de-facto team leader' emerges as the one that team coaches are in most danger of assuming. Two clear reasons for this emerge – one is a sense of being pulled into the role due to a perceived vacuum with a lack of strong leadership in the team.

Grace acknowledges how she was pulled into the team leader role, as well as the signs that she was starting to assume the role.

> 'The pseudo team leadership role – I've done that as well! That's a natural position for me. It's when you feel as if there's a bit of a vacuum there. Usually the team leader is not doing it or doesn't really know how to do it.'

The second reason relates to the team coach's own background – the fact that they have led large senior teams in the past and the team leader role feels natural and comfortable. Here, there is more of a sense of push from the team coach, them getting overly involved and starting to assume the leader role.

An example of this was provided by Jackie, who somewhat jokingly remarked, 'Well, I'm the leader, the director of the day! I'm directing the orchestra, aren't I?' before pausing to reflect and adding, 'That's a comfortable role; a bit too comfortable, really…'

Jackie's comment raises an underlying ethical issue around boundaries, working with the team leader rather than taking on that role, and the team coach being attuned to their own needs and areas of comfort, as well as aware of the various hooks that might draw them into the leader role. An example of this in action was provided by Kennedy, who described her own background and comfort areas: 'I've run all the versions, huge multi-million organisations. I'd be very happy leading.' However, she recognised the danger of 'making myself bigger than the leader', continuing to muse, '...and then, what happens when I leave? I need to work with the leader to keep them big, while I need to be small'.

Kennedy noticed behaviours from team members that indicated she was getting drawn into being their leader: 'Looking to me rather than at each other. That's the first sign.' Continuing her story, she described behaviours she adopted to halt this pattern:

'I invite them to look at each other when
they're talking rather than at me. I always try
to sit a little bit further back. Because initially,
when I first started out, I was sitting with
them, and then it would naturally happen.
I found myself sitting further and further back
so that I would be out of it, but if they kept
talking to me, then I would invite them to look
at each other.'

Parenting roles

The theory of TA was developed by Eric Berne in the 1950s (Berne, 1959). In essence, Berne suggested that when we communicate with others, we do so from one of three ego states: parent, adult or child.

The parent ego state utilises attitudes and behaviour patterns, borrowed or modelled, which resemble those of a parental figure. When we are in parent state, we can behave in two ways – critical or nurturing. This state comes from our experiences of life, particularly early life, with our parents and teachers. When we feel, think, talk and behave in the way we remember our parents doing, then we are adopting a parent state.

The child ego state utilises attitudes and behaviour patterns which are relics of our own childhood. In child state, we can also act in one of two ways – free child or adapted child. Free child is categorised by impulsive, instinctive, creative, undisciplined and, at times, demanding behaviour. Adapted child is when we carry the influences of our upbringing, for example doing as we are told, into the present day.

The adult ego state utilises feelings, attitudes and behaviour patterns which are adapted to our current reality. In essence, it is us operating in the present, here and now. The adult ego is the mature and deliberating part of our personality. When we are in adult state, our actions and words are well considered – in contrast to the almost automatic reactions of the parent or child states.

The team coaches I interviewed in my study (Graves, 2021) were familiar with TA, so it was not surprising that there were a significant number of references to ego states, especially critical and nurturing parent, and to team coaches being 'hooked' or 'triggered' into different roles by team members' behaviour. The nurturing parent ego state was widely cited as a role team coaches were aware that they moved into, with some aspects of it regarded as positive. For Jackie, nurturing parent had a valid role in ensuring that no one on the team was talked over and that 'everyone's voice is heard'.

The challenge appeared to be when the team coach became too drawn into the nurturing parent ego state or found themselves in 'rescuer' role. Consistent terms they used to describe this sense of being too involved included 'feeling sorry' for team members, or a desire to 'help out', 'look after' or 'sort it out for' them.

Almost the same number of examples of being triggered into critical parent were provided as being pulled into nurturing parent, as can be seen below.

Critical parent examples in action

I got hooked into Sam's 'no time, this is stupid' comments during the crowd surfing exercise. I went to the critical parent and stopped everyone to announce that Sam wanted more time. It was an attempt to embarrass her, but she wasn't, and they continued on. (Bob)

Sometimes I can get the controlling parent turning up, versus noticing that I'm getting frustrated, so needing to be very calm, 'it's OK, you're not their parent, you're not the team leader'. (Kennedy)

By the end of it I'm thinking, 'how long do you carry on calling it out?'. How long do you just say, 'OK we've had two hours where nobody's called anything out', but I've noticed it happen! I find this quite difficult as a team coach because, actually, I just feel myself getting frustrated and I need to manage myself to not become too parent-like and start treating them like children. (Liza)

I have fallen into controlling parent, and it really doesn't feel like it fits me. I feel like it lands really badly, it sounds like I'm being really clipped and it's not really me. Unfairness, people not listening, imbalance, lack of consideration. They're my main triggers. (Jackie)

Nurturing parent examples in action

I was aware of the dynamic and wanted to look after him, but also felt loyal to the team and didn't want him to skew things. So, I was aware of feeling a bit parental in that space and that pull that you feel as a parent sometimes. (John)

If I go into parent role, it tends to be nurturing parent. If someone is talked over, I want to make sure their voice is heard. (Jackie)

I think I've been sucked into being overly supportive of the team you know, 'it really is tough for you guys', and I've become a nurturing parent. 'Don't worry, Liza will look after it.' (Liza)

Mother, that caring, holding, but I think that when it becomes too parent/child, it can be dangerous. I sense that coming in, that wanting to help out and sort everything out. That nurturing parent, sort them out, help them. (Kennedy)

Sometimes you just have to be explicit with team leaders and tell it how you see it. I'm getting more comfortable with that. It's me watching when the child comes out. How do I respond and stay in my role? (Anita)

She was looking at me beseechingly, 'what the hell do I do here?'. And I was torn… I did feel sorry for her, that she had everything against her. He was older, higher up the tree, there was a male/female dynamic… There was a lot going on that made it difficult for her. I put them together, so I felt responsible as well. (Grace)

In terms of their experiences of being pulled into the two roles, team coaches' responses are spread across a spectrum. At one end of the spectrum are those who identify strongly with nurturing parent. They emphasise the building psychological safety and relationships aspects of team coaching and express some discomfort in challenging individuals in a group setting. In the middle are those who recognise that they could be pulled into either nurturing parent or critical parent, depending on the situation and particular triggers. At the other end of the spectrum are those who only identify with critical parent. It is notable that this group prefers some of the stronger forms of challenge.

While some aspects of nurturing parent can be regarded as beneficial, critical parent is presented in a negative light. An example of being triggered by team members' behaviour and reacting in a way the team coach then regretted was provided by Joy. Reflecting on a challenging session, she wrote:

> 'In the large group, the three girls formed a
> clique and were vocal with personal agendas.
> I had to shut them down at one point as it was
> going off topic, which made them sulk like
> school kids! I went into parent role and got
> sulky child reaction.'

Joy reflected upon how she had taken this particular team coaching session to supervision and concluded that she 'didn't handle it elegantly and it was like corralling school kids all morning'. Reflecting on the next team coaching session, Joy noted how she had taken the learning from this session and 'softened the tone', using more of a 'how shall we approach this?' style which resulted in more positive behaviours.

In my own study (Graves, 2021), most of the examples provided by team coaches of being drawn into nurturing or critical parent roles were taken from reflective logs or discussion during focus groups, rather than interviews. This would suggest that these dynamics of transference and countertransference are not generally in the conscious awareness of the team coach.

Thornton (2019a) concurs with this view, posing the questions, 'who or what am I invited to be?' and 'what feelings do you have in the room/are you left with afterwards?', encouraging the coach to reflect upon their own 'bodily and emotional responses' alongside their 'thinking to understand what is going on' (p 216). All of this highlights that engaging in reflective practice and supervision is important for the team coach in noticing how their work is affecting them, as well as any patterns they are falling into. This theme is picked up and expanded upon in Chapter Six.

This chapter has explored the importance and various ways of creating the container of support and challenge in which the team coaching work takes place. It has reviewed the range of roles that the team coach may adopt during interventions – both those that they choose to adopt and those they are drawn into. Throughout the chapter, I have identified some of the various and often very different ways in which practising team coaches create safety, provide challenge and utilise different roles.

As with so many aspects of team coaching, there is no best or model practice, and so I have deliberately avoided attempting to provide one. Instead, I have captured some of the key considerations for team coaches to reflect upon as they engage in team coaching in the table in this chapter, and also in The PiE Team Coaching Model® Framework in Appendix A.

In the next chapter, we will explore what actually takes place in team coaching, including the range of practices and activities used by team coaches.

My experience of team coaching...

Plans
Not perfect
Better, uncertain, pride
Let them
Stand-back

— *Joy*

FOUR

Intervention – What Do Team Coaches *Actually* Do In Sessions?

W hen we are seeking to understand where team coaching is in its emergence as a practice, the development of its older and more mature sibling, individual coaching, provides a useful comparison. Bachkirova and Kauffman (2009) argue that there is a wide range of perspectives on what individual coaching is and it is the richness of these perspectives that contributes to the development of the field. Bachkirova and Kauffman conclude that approaches to coaching are diverse and definitions seem to be evolving, although each coach has some internal working definition of what he or she offers.

A more recent comprehensive review of the coaching process concluded that the coaching landscape has not become significantly clearer, with a diversity of definitions and styles being adopted (Myers, 2017). If this is the case, then logic would suggest that there would be even less clarity surrounding team coaching, which has been described on multiple occasions in this book as a largely young and emergent process. This lack of development is evident in the different ways in which team coaches define the practice, the diversity of approaches they adopt, interventions they make and how they describe their sessions.

As stated in Chapter One, it is possible to identify some universality of experience relating to elements of team coaching that are present in all types, genres and approaches to it. These elements are:

- It is a process that takes place over a number of sessions, spread out over a period of time.

- It involves individuals in a team learning together while completing a task/carrying out their business.

- It is holistic, focusing on the whole team.

- It involves work that necessitates use of a coach (ie it is not simply team building).

- It focuses on the health of the team and long-term change, utilising the behaviours and skills of individual coaching.

While there is convergence on the above elements of team coaching, there is significant divergence on other aspects of the process – which is not that helpful for those trying to understand the process and, perhaps more significantly, what happens in team coaching sessions. What does a team coach actually do? What activities and practices does the team engage in? A useful framing for understanding these differences is that they can be seen to fall into three types of divergence: theoretical/philosophical perspectives; personality differences; and developmental aspects.

This chapter explores how these three different types of divergence influence how the team coach works with a team, including the ways of working and activities that they gravitate towards or avoid. Throughout the chapter, I have used the words of various team coaches to illustrate points, describe the work they have undertaken and provide an insight into the rich landscape of activities and ways of working which take place under the umbrella of team coaching.

Theoretical/philosophical perspectives

Team coaches tend to bring whatever theoretical/philosophical perspective they utilise in their individual coaching practice into their team coaching work – for example, Gestalt, person-centred, systemic and TA – and these divergent philosophical perspectives are evident in the approaches they adopt and the interventions they subsequently make. The person-centred coach will focus on creating a growth-promoting climate to bring about change, with challenge taking the form of light-touch observational feedback to raise awareness, whereas the systemic coach will adopt approaches involving the wider system, including use of constellation activities. A useful introduction to how theoretical/philosophical perspectives influence coaching style is provided in *The Complete Handbook of Coaching* (Cox, Bachkirova and Clutterbuck, 2023), with separate chapters describing Gestalt, TA, existential, positive psychology, solution-focused and cognitive behavioural.

For those who appreciate examples of how theory translates into practice, below are the words of two team coaches, describing how their own theoretical perspective and development influence their team coaching practice. Kennedy describes the systemic approach in action, while Anita describes how as a Gestalt coach, she favours interventions that heighten team members' awareness of their here-and-now communication, including creative approaches.

The systemic approach in action (Kennedy)

'If I think of my systemic training, as a systemic coach, I use myself as a barometer to pick up what's going on in the room. Is there anger, anxiety, happiness? I feed that back as "Is this me or am I actually holding it for the team?" The same is true in how I think of a metaphor and then offer this to the team. It's just a picture that I'm getting – it might be useful, it might not be, but it might give them some clarity or something to work on, or think about their own metaphor. I might say, "What would your metaphor be, individually and as a team?"

'I'm interested from a systemic point of view in how the position that somebody might play, or how long they've been in the team, affects the team dynamic. I often bring that into my team coaching by using constellation activities – for example, inviting team members to stand in order of who joined the organisation first, or who joined the team first – because sometimes, teams are already established. You don't necessarily have the luxury of joining the team when it's just starting.'

A Gestalt-based approach in action (Anita)

'I'm definitely influenced by Gestalt. It suits my intuitive style, just being in the present, observing what's emerging, helping clients to be present – "What are you experiencing now?" I'm interested in the spiritual side of things: energy, holism, etc. I've come to understand that all the principles are the same and I would describe Gestalt as a spiritual practice. It's noticing what's emerging for me – is this about me or is there something useful here that I can bring in? That's how I like to work and I have a whole toolkit of stuff now, including constellations, embodiment, the somatic stuff that really interests me. I encourage drawing and writing.

'There was a time when I'd learn a new technique and think, "How can I bring it in?" but now I'm noticing that I'm not actually using a lot of that stuff. I might have the theory in my head – say, "immunity to change" and Prochaska would be frameworks that I'd be aware of, but my client wouldn't know. In the past, I'd have taken them out and shown the client and talked them through these frameworks, whereas now I try to stay present with them. I do that in my one-to-one and team coaching.

'I tend to give clients frameworks to hang on to in the circle conversations. I call it the "discovery piece" – raising the awareness of what is, and then having the conversation around what they need to talk about.'

The theoretical/philosophical perspective of the team coach can, therefore, be seen to have a significant influence on their practice, but it is by no means the only influence.

Personality differences

Another way of looking at different approaches to team coaching is whether these are structured and planned or more emergent (Clutterbuck et al, 2019; Lawrence et al, 2019). Clutterbuck et al differentiate between 'fluid' and 'rigid' approaches, with the former aiming to give as much control over the learning dialogue as possible to the team. Examples of fluid approaches in action can be seen when Bob and Kennedy describe their typical coaching sessions:

'A workshop has a rough agenda. We will always spend time thinking about what we're going to do. Also, it is flexible – it's part of the skill of a team coach, knowing how to hold the tension between "here's the next thing to do" versus "something's happening right now". How do you hold both those things? For me, it's always about offering the menu back to the team while having my own view and sharing that. I don't usually send the agenda out in advance – it's often flip charted on the day.' (Bob)

'I have some ideas on what has happened in the previous session, but I always turn up with those in my back pocket. I ask, "Where are you? What's going on? What's going to be useful for you today?" Usually, it is some sort of immediate issue that has happened the day before or last week, or something the team members are working on that they need to get together on for the next couple of weeks.' (Kennedy)

By contrast, more structured approaches often start with all members of the team undertaking the same diagnostics to determine the issues the coaching will focus on or completing the same psychometric assessment. Examples of structured approaches come from John and Joy:

'In practice, I love the Jungian Type approach, so I tend to start with or bring that in somewhere – usually near the beginning. Often using the MBTI as a way in, but not always. That's part of my, if you like, normal way of working with people.' (John)

'At the start, we'll run at least one psychometric, DISC or strengths questionnaire, and depending on how long the team's been together will determine whether we do a team diagnostic at the same time.' (Joy)

Different approaches to planning and structure prevail with some team coaches describing a typical team coaching assignment in detail, whereas others tend to describe the first session and a sense of how an assignment might then evolve. My own study (Graves, 2021) provided some additional insight that much of this difference in approach is driven by personality preferences. Team coaches who identified as favouring a planned and structured approach described how they adopted this approach in their work in general, including in their individual coaching. Even when they had ostensibly turned up without a plan for a team coaching session, they had something in their back pocket. Conversely, those who favoured a more spontaneous approach were similarly consistent in how they applied this – using little structure and planning in their individual coaching sessions and having a strong preference for seeing what emerged in team coaching sessions.

Personality differences were also evident in the language team coaches used to describe themselves. On occasion, these personality traits were vocalised at an identity level, for example, 'I'm provocative' or 'I'm not a challenging coach'. It was then apparent that this sense of self translated into the coach's behaviours, with 'I'm provocative' readily providing examples of their high challenge interventions and 'I'm not a challenging coach' describing a reluctance to directly challenge and instead providing examples of observational feedback. Some part of the difference in approaches and interventions in team coaching, therefore, appears to be due to personality preferences.

Developmental differences

My own route to team coaching has been via many years of individual coaching. Likewise, the team coaches that I have spoken to as part of my research have been highly experienced individual coaches with varying levels of experience of team coaching. Some had undertaken qualifications in team coaching, whereas others had not.

The existing literature provides a helpful starting point for how this difference may manifest itself in team coaching, with Hackman and Wageman (2005) identifying one form of team coaching as 'eclectic', and Clutterbuck (2008) suggesting that there are two categories of team coaches. Coaches in the first category transfer what they do when coaching individuals and 'add a dash of facilitation and/or team building, and then wing it' (p 220). Those in the second, he argues, start from a deep understanding of process and team dynamics, distinguish carefully between team coaching and team facilitation, and have clarity on practical and ethical issues. Clutterbuck argues that there are more coaches in the first category than the second.

I would certainly concur that team coaches lean heavily on their individual coaching practice, but my own experience suggests that Clutterbuck's two categories are too polarised and do not take sufficient account of the many shades of grey in between. There is certainly some evidence that those who have undertaken team coaching development make decisions relating to their practice, particularly around ethical and boundary issues – for example, providing individual coaching alongside team coaching. However, it is also notable that team coaches do not arrive at the same conclusions with differing practices in place.

It could certainly be argued that additional team coaching development currently appears to provide more theoretical knowledge and awareness of some of the dilemmas, but not necessarily a ready solution to ethical considerations for team coaches. However, as the nature, context, content and skills base for team coaching continue to evolve, good practice and standards are starting to emerge from the professional coaching bodies, in particular the Association of Coaching Supervisors and the European Mentoring and Coaching Council.

The structure of a 'typical' team coaching assignment

The team coach's own theoretical/philosophical perspective on coaching, personality preferences and CPD will impact on how they work with the team and the kinds of activities they choose to engage with or not. One way of appreciating how these ingredients translate into team coaching practice is hearing how three different experienced team coaches describe their approach to a 'typical' team coaching assignment.

Team Coach A (Bob)

'In terms of structure, I'd look for a six- to nine-month engagement, usually four workshops, a day long at a time, starting off with a contracting meeting with the team lead, then a contracting meeting with the team itself to determine their vision of success, what they want to get out of the engagement, confidentiality, diagnostics, what I expect of them, what they expect of me, what they think team coaching is and isn't. Then there'd be a diagnostic phase, both meeting one-to-one and as an online survey.

'Another philosophy is "there are two of us". In 99% of interventions there are two coaches on the basis that we will provide a range of personalities, experiences, insights, four eyes are better than two. It gives the team members someone different to connect with and different role models.

'Part of my process would be to give the team leader a quick snapshot of the initial diagnostic results before the first debriefs – so they don't get alarmed or surprised by anything. Just quickly – not the full story, because I want them to experience the session with the team as opposed to being pre-armed. Things like "Your ratings are different to the team's", "You've been mentioned here quite a bit – how are you going to deal with that?" or "How can I support you on the day? How do you and I stay connected?" to get them settled in.

'The first workshop is usually around debriefing the data in the morning, picking

up some norms before that, then using the
afternoon to get the participants to start
focusing on where they want to focus,
checking on progress, contracting for the next
intervention. A rhythm of a workshop is like
a check-in call – "How's it going? What do
you as a team want to address in the next
workshop?" and so on.'

Team Coach B (Liza)

'Typically, a team coaching assignment is
four to six sessions – if I get four sessions,
I'm happy, but ideally I'd want six. A session
can often be a day. The morning will be the
participants having a normal team meeting,
and then in the afternoon we'll be working on
something specific, but I'm sometimes there as
a facilitator in the morning to try to help them
understand what's happening. Other times,
I'm just there to observe what's happening
and play it back to them later. I don't suppose
there really is a "typical" assignment, but
ideally, I want a combination of observing
them, facilitating them, coaching them, but
everything has to be stuff that they need to
work on in the business so they're working on
themselves and the business at the same time.

'Recently, I've been using the Team Accelerator
Model. That starts off with a diagnostic of

how the team members see themselves, how their commissioner sees them and how the stakeholders see them, and we're looking at several areas. We're looking at what it is that they are there to deliver – that is, how they're structured, what is unique to them and how clear they are on their direction – so we're looking at the business. Then there's a bit about how they organise themselves – how they are internally organised. Have they got the best people for the jobs? Have they got the right skills for what's needed in the future? We've then also got a bit around how they integrate with the rest of the business, their stakeholder management, their eye on the future.

'The middle section is all about their sustainability – how do they look after themselves as a team? How do they let new people in? It's the wellbeing of the team, so basically we get the diagnostic against those things using scores. That gets shown to the team leader, or the manager of the team, and maybe with some stakeholder interviews and anything that the leader's got (they might have their own 360s, whatever), it is a full-day workshop looking at all that data together. Given that data, what does the team want to work on? Where do they want to start? If they don't have a purpose, that's usually a pretty good place to start.'

Team Coach C (Grace)

'I start with having a conversation with whoever first enquired about coaching, the initial stakeholder. My next step is usually to propose a fairly loose framework of potential activities based on what it is that they sound like they're looking for. That may include initial one-to-one conversations with the team members; it may or may not include some kind of psychometric for the team to get to know themselves better; it may or may not include some kind of team-effectiveness assessment tool, a session around them contracting and getting on the same page on why we're doing what we're doing, then an action planning process to say, "OK, these are the areas we want to work on – how are we going to do that?"

'The middle bit can be quite loose and hard to define at the beginning, and then there's usually something at the end as a closing activity: "What have we achieved? What's the distance travelled? Where do you go next as I hand you back to yourselves to self-manage?" That sense of a beginning, a middle and an end to it – I guess I've got a fairly macro picture in my head of what it might look like.

'The team coaching sessions I've done have usually been over a six- to twelve-month period, in which time I might have done four or five team sessions. I usually plan for sessions to be three hours, but sometimes, if clients are really short of time, I will do two hours. There may also be individual sessions along the way that either I've done or other coaches have supported.'

Team coaching tools and techniques

One of the distinctive features of team coaching, when compared to other team interventions, is that it constitutes a number of sessions, most commonly between four and six. While the above paragraphs describe in-depth interventions that team coaches use, including psychometrics, surveys, creating a team vision and values, etc, team coaches generally use shorter ad hoc activities during sessions. The list of those is extensive and the team coaches I spoke to described just some of them below.

Creative tools and techniques

'It's handy to have different techniques when participants get stuck, like constellations or Gestalt chair exercises – things that get them up and moving, and being comfortable with that – or creative exercises, using cards – things that get them thinking differently. With some groups, I might do mindfulness and principles of meditation if it feels appropriate.' (Anita)

Use of metaphor

'I love using metaphors and offering these to the team. For example, I'll say, "I got this image as you were talking of being at the start of a synchronised swimming routine, for some reason. How far away are you from the group and how long do you have to swim to get to them? Do you have the right swimsuit on? Are you carrying weights?" That is my metaphor – how do we get the team to do a synchronised swim?

'That's quite difficult because it relies on what's going on underneath the surface, what we see and what we don't see. My purpose is to offer what I'm sensing and feeling and see if it resonates. For some it lands and for others it doesn't, so they're not really attached to it if it doesn't land. My offering any metaphor is to see whether it's useful to them. Is it in the room?' (Kennedy)

Use of models and theory

'Sometimes, I see something going on, and this usually happens when I'm the second coach and I'm observing the first coach with the group. For example, the parent/child. I then step in, asking, "Would this be useful? There's a well-known model that might explain…"

'For me, the whole purpose of sharing something like that is to try to normalise what's happening. For example, quite often I put into a contract the Support and Challenge model because I tend to find I keep coming back to that if somebody attacks a team member.

'The other thing is when the participants are despondent because all the changes they're trying to put into place aren't working and everybody's blaming them, I say, "That's brilliant, that's progress" and remind them of the change curve. Because my mind tends to think like this, the models really help my thinking when I'm trying to normalise stuff for them.' (Liza)

Gestalt and somatic techniques:

'If we're thinking about what the team purpose is, I often include the chair exercise. I add an extra chair representing team purpose because I want the participants to always remember that there is only one reason why we are spending the day together: in service of that team purpose and the stakeholders. Team members take it in turns to sit on the chair that represents the true purpose and experience that perspective.

'Another exercise could be around John Gottman's Four Horsemen – criticism, defensiveness, stonewalling, contempt. I get team members to experience each of these four team toxins, to embody it, then ask, "What position would you take? What would your body language be like if you were defensive or stonewalling?" Eventually, I get them into the position of the one that they know they're most likely to do, and I ask them to talk to each other using language as if they were, for example, stonewalling each other.

'Then I ask them to stand in the team toxin that they would be least comfortable being confronted with. It's always me asking questions or making suggestions, like: "How did that feel?" or "Talk to each other like this…" or "What are you noticing?" I always use questions, but we do a mixture of sitting down and standing up.' (Monica)

Team development and effectiveness theory

'I'll always introduce Tuckman with team members and I usually send them Lencioni's forty-minute keynote on YouTube, which talks through it [the Five Dysfunctions of a Team], because it's really engaging. They get it and have a rich understanding of trust in conversations.' (Joy)

Team activities

In my own practice, I invariably find myself using the Team Issues Table (see the illustration below). This invites team members to focus on three kinds of issues facing the team:

- Issues 1: Those on the table that are being resolved, all team members are aware of them and are acting upon them.

- Issues 2: Those on the table that are not being addressed or resolved. Team members are aware of them and there is some open discussion, but so far no plan of action for resolving them.

- Issues 3: Issues under the table. Some team members are aware of them, whereas some are not aware or don't consider them true issues. The issues are sensitive to some team members, not openly discussed and not being resolved.

I often use this table at some stage during a team coaching assignment. I find it is useful for providing the participants with a framework to have some open conversations about what is known/unknown in the team and what is currently being acted upon / ignored. It is a really flexible exercise and can be used as individual prework ahead of sessions or worked on by the team as a whole in a session. My personal preference is to have a huge mock-up of the table in the room and get team members off their chairs, engaging with the issues and discussing these with their colleagues.

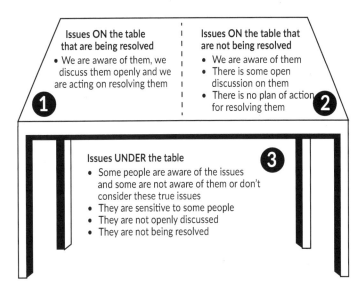

Team Issues Table

Diverse team coaching approaches

At the start of this chapter, I referenced Bachkirova and Kauffman (2009) on the different perspectives on individual coaching. They complete their critique by concluding that one argument is to:

'...abandon the criterion of universality and accept that there could be as many types of coaching as there are individual coaches.' (Bachkirova and Kauffman, 2009, p 107)

An extension of this argument would suggest that the degree of divergence for team coaching will be considerably greater than for individual coaching, taking into account the additional experiences team coaches will be bringing from working with groups and teams as well as further development they may have undergone. The lists below of 'typical' approaches and variations capture just some of the diverse range of activities undertaken by team coaches in their work, with references for these tools and techniques provided in Appendix C. What emerges from this review of approaches is a sense of there being no best way or one size fits all, and that effective team coaching conversations balance structure (a broad and purposeful framework) and flow (dealing with issues, ideas and insights as they occur) (Hodge and Clutterbuck, 2019).

Most frequently used psychometrics, frameworks, models and tools

- Jungian 'type': The Myers-Briggs Type Indicator®, Insights Discovery® or DISC®

- Strengths questionnaires (eg Strengthscope, StrengthsFinder)

- Establishing team purpose, team charter and values

- Lencioni's Five Dysfunctions of a Team

Additional questionnaires, frameworks, models and tools used

- Team Accelerator Model

- TCI Team Diagnostic™

- TDS

- Team surveys designed by team coach, pulled from various sources

- The Rocket Model™

- Tuckman – theory of developmental sequences in small groups

- Leadership Climate Indicator

- The Hogan Team Report

- Neuro Linguistic Programming (NLP)

- EBW Global Emotional Intelligence

- Clean Language Methodology

- Support and Challenge Model

- Proschaska's Stages of Change

- Change Curve

- Immunity to Change

- Gestalt chair exercises

- Systemic constellations

- Embodiment exercises, eg using Gottman's Four Horsemen

- Mindfulness and principles of meditation

This chapter has explored some of the convergences and divergences in team coaching practice and how these are affected particularly by theoretical/philosophical perspectives, personality preferences and professional development. The next chapter will move on to the final phase of team coaching, the Evaluation phase.

My experience of team coaching...

Reward
Knowledge transfer
Like-minded people
Build capability
Success

— *Jen*

FIVE

Evaluation

The process of Evaluation is represented in the third and final phase of The PiE Team Coaching Model®. This is the time for the team coach to take stock, evaluating the work that they have undertaken on behalf of the client, including their performance as a team coach, as well as understanding what they are taking away from the work and bringing the assignment to a clear ending.

As already described in previous chapters, the nature, context, content and skills base for team coaching are still evolving and competency frameworks and standards are emerging. As such, it is somewhat inevitable that the final stage of the process, evaluating its success, remains a work in progress. At a simplistic level, this can be seen in the brevity of this chapter when compared with the Preparation and Intervention chapters.

This chapter will explore some of the current practices for evaluating the success of team coaching, including the use of objective and subjective criteria, as well as perspectives on indicators that team coaching is not working. Throughout the chapter, I will draw heavily on my own research and use the voices of team coaches to describe their current and emerging evaluation practices.

Evaluating my team coaching work

In Chapter One, we explored how much of the literature on team coaching focuses on attempts to define it as a discrete process and different to other team interventions, for example facilitation and team building. My conclusion, based on my experience as a practitioner, as well as in-depth discussions with other team coaches, is that team coaching is a discrete process while I acknowledge somewhat 'fuzzy' boundaries between it and other team interventions. As such, I would argue that an important part of the Evaluation phase is the coach's own self-reflection, including reflecting on the work they have undertaken under the umbrella of team coaching, and whether it was indeed team coaching or something else that they delivered.

When we are evaluating what exactly team coaching is, it often appears easier to describe what it is not. In my conversations with team coaches, similar expressions were used to describe what team coaching is not, including any intervention seen as 'team building', getting team members together to have a 'nice day' or 'fun', and work with a 'short-term focus'. For some team coaches, an understanding of what team coaching is often emerges as they reflect on work they have been involved in previously which they now conclude was not team coaching. This work might have been sold, by themselves or others, as team coaching, but in hindsight, it was largely facilitation or training.

Joy pulled together these elements in her summary:

> 'Anything which is seen as a team build
> event isn't team coaching. I mean the piece
> where we're not looking at any longer-term
> behavioural change, where we're only looking
> at the output rather than the health of the team.
> If we're just going to get everyone together to
> have a nice day, then I would say it's not even
> group coaching; it's pure facilitation.'

In hindsight, team coaches reflected on 'team coaching' work that they had undertaken, but they had adopted approaches that had been too interventionist and theory-driven, and any improvements were probably short-lived. As someone who had recently completed a team coaching diploma, having been practising team coaching for some time before, Kennedy provided an insight into her transition into team coaching and growing awareness of what it is/is not:

> 'I thought I was doing team coaching, but in fact, I was just facilitating... I was brought in as the "expert" to sort the team out versus supporting them to support themselves...

> 'There have been some positive experiences before, but I realise they weren't team coaching. People have gained a lot of benefit from sitting talking; some of the facilitation I've done or some of the input I've given around theories has been really useful, but it wasn't coaching!'

While there was convergence among the team coaches I spoke to on the kinds of activities that are not team coaching, there was also divergence, some of which we explored in the previous chapter. For example, some team coaches routinely work with a team on their charter, vision, purpose, and use psychometrics to provide a common language and understanding for the team, describing these activities as a core part of team coaching and often the starting point for the work. For others, the use of tools and techniques can result in a perception that the work focuses too much on process.

At first sight, this appears a somewhat confusing land-scape with some clear agreement on what does/does not constitute team coaching as well as some distinct disagreements. What is evident from my conversations with practitioners is that team coaches are generally quite clear about what constitutes team coaching *for them* and also know when they are straying or being drawn into something that they do not recognise as team coaching.

While a more in-depth review of reflection as part of supervision is covered in the next chapter, self-reflec-tion and, if applicable, peer reflection with a co-coach is important to engage in at the end of an assignment to enable the coach to evaluate their own performance and extract any learning for their ongoing develop-ment. Was I/were we team coaching or something else based on my/our criteria? What do I/we need to be mindful of in future?

Evaluating the success of team coaching

Team coaching is typically a lengthy and expensive development intervention, particularly if all aspects of the process are included: gathering insight from team members and stakeholders, working with a co-coach, carrying out a number of sessions and possibly including some individual coaching. To date, no study has been undertaken to compare the costs and benefits of team coaching versus individual coaching of team members, but it might be expected that the costs per head would be lower and the impact higher (Clutterbuck and Graves, 2023). The stakes are, therefore, high to demonstrate that such a significant investment in time and money works.

The challenge of evaluating the success of team coaching is one that I have wrestled with in my own practice as well as exploring in my research. In a recent study (Graves, 2021), one of the questions I asked team coaches in interviews and focus groups was 'How do you know your team coaching is working?'

It is notable that team coaches used consistent terms to describe their current evaluation process, including 'emergent', 'embryonic' and 'anecdotal'. In addition, when describing current processes that they had in place, they often used caveats, and descriptions lacked detail of the rigour applied.

A common practice involves rerunning surveys/ questionnaires used at the start of the assignment to demonstrate progress. Grace describes this practice, although her choice of words and tone suggest that she is less than convinced about its true worth.

'I suppose at what is a fairly superficial level...
you might do some team-effectiveness measure
and you might measure it again later, and then
say, "Actually, I think we have made progress
on those specific things".'

For Bob, his evaluation is similarly 'anecdotal at the moment', comprising a rerun of a survey, but complementing this with feedback, for example, 'team members saying that they've gained something from it in terms of clarity or the ability to have tougher conversations or greater trust in the team'.

Yet surveys can be problematic to rerun as scores can go down as well as up. As someone who regularly reruns a survey, either the whole survey or a pulse check on a number of factors, Liza explains how scores often go down before they start to improve, as 'what typically happens is the team members are harder on themselves because they now know what "good" looks like'. While Liza argues how this can be an excellent learning experience for the team, she also volunteers:

> '…it takes a bit of realisation for them to think, "It's not because we're worse; we are actually better, but we now know what we're striving towards". For example, they'll say they've managed their stakeholders brilliantly, they've had some feedback from the stakeholders saying they haven't, and now they see what they don't do".'

While this increasing self-awareness on the part of the team is useful, managing the narrative for team members, and potentially stakeholders, around a set of scores which have apparently worsened as a result of team coaching needs some skill, experience and perhaps bravery on the part of the team coach.

How do I know team coaching is working?

For most team coaches, assessing how well the team coaching is going appears to be largely down to their own intuition, sometimes aided by a key moment in a specific session when there was a notable shift in the room. Asked to provide examples of this, some team coaches could recall exact moments in rich detail.

For Bob, this moment happened in workshop three when one of the team members said:

> 'When we meet, there's no fun anymore.
> I come protecting myself and it's not fun.
> There's no energy, and yet the very thing we
> should be focusing on is how we bring energy
> to our 300 reports.'

Looking back, Bob says that was 'the moment when something moved for one person first, then it moved others'. For Kennedy, the shift happened during the fourth session when she observed that team members were able to be 'quite vulnerable with each other' during a lengthy difficult conversation:

> 'After that meaningful conversation, they were
> almost flying. It was like they had to unpack a
> lot of layers and hit rock bottom to then fly…
> carry each other up.'

Kennedy similarly recognised a shift in behaviour from the team leader. In the initial sessions, she noted how he'd always asked her, 'What should I do?' but in the later sessions, 'it was he who was making the decisions'. She recollected a specific occasion when the leader had made a decision:

> 'My personal satisfaction was, "Yes! He's owning it!" I fed back to him that there was a real shift in his authority towards me, and towards the other team members in his authority as a leader. It was great to witness that.'

However, change does not always entail a discernible shift in the room at a specific moment in time, with team coaches often describing noticing more subtle changes in team members' ways of being and acting. The team coaches I spoke to used consistent language to recognise such behaviour, including 'energy in the room', team members being 'comfortable disagreeing with each other', 'challenging each other' and having 'productive' conversations about the 'real issues'.

Another key aspect of evaluating the success of team coaching is the sustainability of the work during the remainder of the intervention, but also crucially beyond the life of the assignment. Recalling her work with one team, Kennedy reflected on how she became aware of team members sharing more of their experiences, listening and connecting with each other and showing a lot more empathy. She sensed that the change was becoming embodied:

> 'You could almost see stronger connections being built as though there were more wires on them… it was like a piece of string, but it was becoming much bigger, a piece of rope. I could sense there was so much more dialogue and openness and sharing.'

Another aspect of sustainability is traction – seeing forward momentum and the team coach is not having to do all the work. For Joy, this is the point where she recognises:

> '…a) they're doing it and b) they're taking accountability for it and challenging each other. At that point, I can step back and I know they're ready. They don't need me anymore. They might want me, but they don't need me. The two are different.'

If evaluating the immediate impact of team coaching is regarded as 'embryonic' and 'anecdotal', then evaluating the longer-term impact can be seen as even more of a challenge and work in progress. Team coaches may identify specific but hard to measure changes they have witnessed, including team members starting to self-facilitate their own meetings going forward; team processes becoming more defined and sharp; and, in particular, action – 'the project gets done or stuff happens, and it happens because they want to get it to happen' (Jackie).

How do I know team coaching is *not* working?

While team coaches might struggle to provide clear, measurable criteria to demonstrate that their team coaching has been a success, they appear to have no such problem in articulating when they know it is not really working. Energy has particular significance and meaning for them, with a high level of energy associated with team coaching working and, conversely, a lack of energy with a sense that it is not working well.

Team coaches describe themselves as being adept at picking up on and interpreting a lack of energy as well as understanding the impact this has on them. For Liza:

> 'I can tell you how I know it's not working!
> It's energy levels at the end of a session.
> I've come out of sessions where energy was
> low, people seemed despondent; they've
> agreed to what they are going to do, and I've
> walked out thinking, "Even they know I'm
> noticing that the energy is low" and "What
> happened there?"'

For Bob, there is a sense of 'stale air' in the room as well as that the 'learning is cut off' and 'people have stayed in their pre-emptive locations or there is no insight or even the conditions for change'. Signs that this is happening are when he feels that teams are going through the motions, there does not appear to be any depth in conversations, and where support is high and challenge low.

Evaluating the success of team coaching, therefore, appears to be in the early stages for team coaches with heavy reliance on their own observations of behavioural changes, levels of energy and activity, as well as some data gathering through rerunning surveys. Practising team coaches appear to be somewhat conflicted by this state of affairs. On the one hand, they all have their own internal barometer to gauge the success of the intervention and do not particularly require further endorsement, but there is a general acceptance that this is not sufficient for stakeholders and potential users of team coaching who would undoubtedly be seeking more tangible measurements of success.

While it can be argued that the same challenges are inherent in individual coaching, team coaching constitutes a significantly greater investment in time and money on the part of organisations and teams, and a lack of clear evaluation criteria and methods is problematic for both practitioners selling team coaching and organisations and teams looking to engage in it. Team coaches appreciate the importance of creating more robust evaluation methods and the evidence suggests that they are in varying stages of seeking to address the issue.

What is apparent is that evaluation needs to be something that the team coach has thought about and discussed with the client at the outset of an assignment, particularly if a pre and post survey is planned. While measurements may be largely subjective and/ or simplistic at present, as team coaching matures as a practice, the demand for more robust success criteria and evaluation methods will undoubtedly increase. I would argue that it is, therefore, incumbent on team coaches to give serious consideration to how they are evaluating their practice and to agree measurements, quantitative and qualitative, at the outset of a team coaching assignment. The key questions for the team coach to ask themselves, the team and stakeholders are provided in the Evaluation section of The PiE Team Coaching Model® Framework in Appendix A.

My experience of team coaching...

Opportunity
Confidence, energy
It gets routine
Overwhelmed, tired
Reflect

— *John*

SIX

Self-care And Supervision

As the body of team coaching literature increases, there is a growing understanding of the dynamic complexity of working with teams rather than individuals and of the need for the team coach to have professional support and supervision (Hodge and Clutterbuck, 2019; Thornton, 2019a; Lawrence, 2019; Graves, 2021). These aspects are captured in The PiE Team Coaching Model®.

The themes of self-care, support and supervision are shown as running throughout an assignment, from Preparation to Evaluation, with different foci of attention in each phase. The related themes of self-care and supervision will be explored in this final chapter.

The importance of self-care

Team coaches describe team coaching as more physically and mentally demanding than individual coaching and evoking a broader range of emotional responses, the highs being higher and the lows being lower. They describe moments of real pride and joy when they have witnessed behavioural changes in team members or the team leader, but they also describe at least as many occasions of self-doubt and anxiety, and how it can be easy to take on the mantle and weight of the pressures of the team.

An example of how coaches experience the difference between individual and team coaching is provided by Jackie:

> 'I need to learn how – and it's true for one-to-one, but it's multiplied in team coaching by how many people are in the room – to bring myself back, because I take a lot on. We have a lot of different roles when we're team coaching. We need to be equipped, learn how to shake off the day without losing the important stuff, but have ourselves mentally cleansed for next time.'

Liza echoed this theme of the team coach continuing to process the work after sessions have finished and this process being far more long-lasting and magnified than for individual coaching:

'I find with team coaching there's so much going on, so many dynamics. I always go away thinking, "Did I do the right thing there?" I probably leave team coaching with more questions about how I behaved than I do in one-to-one sessions. Even with my trickiest one-to-one client, I don't go away and think about it as much as with my team coaching.'

Thornton, writing from a psychodynamic approach to team and group coaching, has long emphasised the challenge of this work, most recently:

'Holding a group of people means containing stronger projections and more difficult feelings than with one person. In working with teams, these stresses (sic) are multiplied because we are also holding the impact of that broader system on the team – all the pressures and "theories-in-use" that organisation members carry with them, particularly the unconscious ones.' (Thornton, 2019b, p 328)

Recent commentary acknowledges the physical and mental complexity of team coaching for the coach (Hodge and Clutterbuck, 2019; Jacox, 2019; Lawrence, 2019; Thornton, 2019a; Thornton, 2019b). This challenge was certainly in evidence in my own research, with team coaches describing the physical and mental demands of the work in rich detail and the importance of establishing self-care practices at the outset of the assignment.

Echoing Thornton, team coaches repeatedly used the analogy of 'holding'. For some, holding is predominantly a mental activity, made more challenging by the numbers of individuals involved:

'When they're all together, it's like, how do you hold all of that? Whereas with one-to-one, it's a lot simpler.' (Jen)

For others, they describe holding what is going on for all individuals in the team in both mental and physical terms:

'It's like in modern dance. There's a sock or very thick tights, and there are two or three people inside it, and you can see an arm pushing out or a head or a leg. It's almost like that's how a team is – they're constantly moving and grappling. The position changes and how they norm and form and perform differently on different days, weeks and months, depending on what's going on for them as a team, individually, in the organisation, in the wider system.' (Kennedy)

At least part of the physical and mental demand of holding team members may be attributed to where the team coach sits in relation to the team. In team facilitation or other team interventions, the person leading the session tends to stand or sit at a slight distance from the team so there is a sense of physical separation and difference, enabling some objectivity. In team coaching, the coach sits alongside members of the team, with most describing a practice of sitting in a circle, opposite and with a clear line of vision to their co-coach if they are working with one, with no tables or other barriers.

The sense of being detached, outside the team in the facilitator role, and in it, sitting with the team as team coach, is depicted in the illustration below.

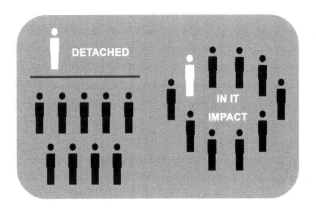

Detached facilitator role versus in it team coach role

Once the team coach is 'in it', the sense of physical distance and difference is lost. The team coach is sitting alongside team members, picking up the same undercurrents, dynamics and emotions, and maintaining objectivity is challenging. While there are benefits of sitting in a circle where there are no barriers and no hierarchies, the practice does require self-awareness and self-management on behalf of the team coach. Team coaches have described the practice as a dance of 'stepping in and stepping out' – being able to get close enough to the team members, but also retain their own sense of self and objectivity.

At its most challenging, the process of holding can be physically and mentally draining. Such an example was provided by Joy, writing in one of her reflective logs at the end of two days' team coaching:

> 'I was knackered at this point, and not picking up on all the clues, so I took a back seat and observed while C facilitated. It was draining, holding all the energies in two days with seventeen people.'

Many of the self-care practices adopted by team coaches have their origin in the Preparation phase of The PiE Team Coaching Model®, namely sharing the load by working with a co-coach, particularly if the team has more than eight members; getting insight from all team members, as well as stakeholders where possible, to avoid getting 'bitten on the bum'; appreciating that the work is demanding, and so allowing for this in the diary and planning sessions – for example, half rather than full days. This is yet another reminder that it is important to take time to work through all aspects of the Preparation checklist and resist the temptation to get going on what might feel like the most interesting aspect of the work: the engagements with the whole team.

Team coaching supervision

Alongside the acknowledgement of the demands of team coaching, the literature has started to address the role of supervision in supporting team coaches (Hodge and Clutterbuck, 2019; Thornton, 2019a; Hodge, 2021). However, the nature of supervision currently provided is highly variable, with some team coaches partaking in regular supervision as part of a particular conceptualisation of team coaching; some currently not taking their team coaching to supervision; while others utilise ad hoc arrangements or adapt current practices. This spectrum is displayed in the illustration below:

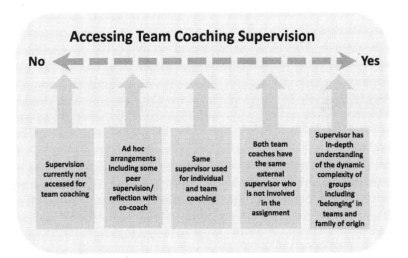

Accessing team coaching supervision

The previous chapters have frequently quoted coaches describing their team coaching practice as 'emergent' or in its 'infancy' and, extending this metaphor, we could argue that team coaching supervision is 'embryonic'. An example of this would be Jackie, speaking from the 'no' end of the spectrum, as she mused out loud in a focus group I was facilitating:

> 'Well… when we've got our own supervisor,
> would we have a team coaching supervisor?
> I was just thinking, I haven't once taken team
> coaching to supervision.'

A common practice is for coaches to use the same supervisor for their individual and team coaching. Several have shared with me how they adopt this practice, occasionally as part of a conscious decision that the supervisor has the experience and knowledge to support both types of work, but for most, this has not been a conscious choice. It has been driven mainly by the fact that it is all 'coaching' work and they have started to incorporate team coaching into existing supervision arrangements.

This approach is exemplified by John:

> 'I have the same supervisor for the whole
> thing. I'm quite comfortable dealing with
> the same person and she seems comfortable
> with it.'

Some coaches have separate team coaching supervision arrangements. An example would be Liza, who described how the methodology she was trained in and follows stipulates that both team coaches share a supervisor who is not involved in the team coaching assignment. Advocating this approach, Liza argued that, while peer reflection with a co-coach is useful, on its own it is not enough:

'I feel quite strongly that there should be an external supervisor involved, otherwise you're both colluding about what a brilliant job – or rubbish job – you do!'

My own study was conducted over a two-year period. As the study progressed, it was evident that team coaches were becoming increasingly aware of the importance of supervision in supporting their team coaching practice. In the initial focus groups and interviews, there had been little mention of supervision, but the role had emerged as a core theme towards the conclusion of the study with rich discussions among team coaches on the form this should take, the types of dilemmas they might take to supervision and the background of the supervisor.

The evidence from this study can be seen to support recent literature that states, as knowledge is gained of the demands of team coaching, the profile of the supervisor is becoming more specific (Hodge and Clutterbuck, 2019; Thornton, 2019b). In their 'Guidelines for team coaching supervision' (2019), Clutterbuck and Hodge argue that coaches need support and challenge that enables them to gain awareness of what might be happening within the whole client system (not just with one individual coachee), and that coaches seek insights from the supervisor about how to balance the purpose and tasks of the coaching while managing the psychological aspects of the team dynamics and relationships.

Thornton (2019a) concurs, describing the role of supervisor as multi-faceted, with supervision used to build confidence and help to prepare and manage ongoing incidents that emerge during the work. She uses the analogy of supervision as providing a 'container' in which the team coach can download their concerns and frustrations, as well as being a safe space for the coach to stand back from and refresh their approaches during a team coaching assignment. To perform such a role, Thornton argues, the supervisor requires specialist knowledge, including experience of working with groups and 'business wisdom'.

In addition, Hodge and Clutterbuck (2019) suggest that insight and learning about the importance and role of supervision can be gained from the neighbouring and more mature discipline of group psychotherapy. One of the benefits of working with a co-coach is often stated as the ability to role model 'teaming' skills in action (Clutterbuck and Graves, 2023), but evidence that this is capitalised on for reflective practice and supervision is weak. Team coaches practising in pairs could benefit from the well-established practice in therapy of having a post session review in which co-therapists provide valuable feedback about each other's behaviour, and also aid each other in the identification and working through of countertransference towards various team members, as well as attending supervision together. Yalom and Leszcz (2005) stress the benefits of co-therapists attending supervision together to provide a 'microcosm' of what happens in group sessions in the form of a parallel process – who defers to whom? Who reports the events of the session? Do the co-therapists compete or complement and build on each other's work, and do they view the group similarly or differently?

Emergent themes in team coaching supervision

Another theme emerging in current commentary is that of team coaches becoming aware of how their own background and needs, family and professional, manifest themselves in their team coaching and the importance of identifying suitable channels to process this insight. Jones (2016) argues that families are our first 'enterprise' and our parents and siblings our first 'management team'. Early family life affects how leaders respond to pressure and react when team members compete for their attention. It influences whether they have close or distant relationships with the people who report to them, communicate directly or indirectly, micromanage or empower, encourage debates or shut them down.

Continuing this theme, Ancona and Perkins (2022) explain the concept of family of origin as, in early life, family dynamics giving rise to many fundamental behaviours and attitudes towards authority and mastery. When similar dynamics emerge at work, people often revert to childhood patterns.

Furthermore, these patterns are not just ghosts lurking at the bottom of the sea; they create hungers that we have to feed and they actively steer us through the world. We bring them to life every day through transference – a process during which thoughts, feelings and responses that have been learned in one setting become activated in another. To enable change, psychologists often encourage clients to consider the nature of their original family system. Ancona and Perkins (2022) argue that, while this approach has been widely applied to behaviours in the personal realm, it can – and should – be applied in the workplace.

Ancona and Perkins identify six elements of family dynamics that commonly play out in the workplace:

- **Values and beliefs** – a shared framework of values and beliefs, unique to the family, determines the shoulds and guides individual behaviour.

- **Roles** – all members in the family tend to play a role, determined in part by their personality and in part by their family system's need for dynamic equilibrium. Common roles include the jester, the troublemaker and the brain.

- **Secrets** – most families have secrets. Sometimes everyone in the family knows them, but they are not shared with outsiders. Other times, only certain people in the family know about them, and those family members hide them from others. Secrets affect how family members communicate and act, and often involve issues that are difficult to acknowledge and discuss.

- **Boundaries**. Families differ significantly in the way in which they think about structure and boundaries. In some families, anything goes; in others, rules are rigid and boundaries maintained. People often find they are more comfortable in organisations that have boundaries like those of their families – large and bureaucratic versus looser and more dynamic.

- **Triangles** are important in determining the dynamics of a family system. Children are masters at the triangle game, often expertly playing one parent off against the other to get what they want. Who forms the three sides in a business setting? What patterns of behaviour dominate?

- **Expectations and mastery**. All parents have expectations of their children. Some children are loyal lieutenants who work hard to live up to these expectations, and in so doing develop a sense of mastery that helps define them as adults. Others try, but fail to meet family expectations and seek out mastery in other ways.

How is this information relevant to the team coach? At one level, it is useful in providing an insight into why team members in coaching sessions might behave in particular ways. From my own experience, one example is a time when I was team coaching and one of the participants turned everything into a joke, using humour throughout the session. Sometimes, this was coarse and felt inappropriate to me, and I noticed other team members wincing or rolling their eyes.

During a coffee break, I decided to raise this privately with the team member and provide some observational feedback. I was cut off mid flow – 'Oh, I've always been like that. I was like it as a child, everyone comments on my humour. I've been told I'm a breath of fresh air in the department.' The lengthier ensuing conversation indicated the role of 'jester' was a very comfortable one for this person.

At a second and deeper level, team coaches do not come to team coaching as a blank canvas. While our education, training and professional experience influence and impact on our development, personal experiences will also have an impact. Indeed, in one study (Campone and Awal, 2012), personal experiences emerged as the most frequently cited influence in a coach's development.

Therefore, self-understanding of our family of origin, and how this has affected who we are as a person and how we show up in a team, is important when we start to work with teams as a team coach. Returning to my own example above, I can see immediately that the role of jester was not one that I adopted as a child and I was brought up with boundaries around humour, what was appropriate and in what context – including coarseness, swearing and behaviour with adults and, in particular, people I did not know well. It is not surprising that I was triggered by this team member's constant use of humour and, in my opinion, inappropriate language, especially in the team coaching setting, as well as the fact that the team leader (the parental figure) did not intervene and call out the behaviour.

In contrast, Kennedy provides an eloquent and compelling account of her own need to belong, driven by a childhood in a single-parent family, with no siblings. Equally, she is aware that she has held some responsible jobs in her time in a corporate setting, and sitting with leaders in a senior team feels comfortable and her rightful place:

'I noticed how comfortable I felt sitting with five other people in a business context because that's where I come from. I felt really comfortable and thought, "Oh, but I don't belong here. I'm only part of this for three hours, and then I leave." My own sense of belonging and not belonging was impacting how I turned up and how I challenged or not, because I was thinking, "This is really lovely, being part of this team."'

For Kennedy – a team coach with a strong systemic background, who has undertaken some personal development in this area – there was some awareness of her own patterns and reactions and how these may show up in a group setting, including her own need to belong and difficulty in saying goodbye. This knowledge led her to realise that it is important she works with a supervisor who has a good understanding of what happens relationally when the coach works with a group, including belonging in teams and the importance of family of origin.

My own research suggests that this level of awareness is by no means universal and team coaches are often taken by surprise in sessions by the strength of their reactions to seemingly innocuous events. Taking time to reflect on our own family of origin, including our responses to Ancona and Perkins' (2022) six factors, and how this affects how we are in groups and teams is certainly a useful activity for practising and aspiring team coaches.

To gain more awareness of patterns and reactions in group settings and how these may be triggered in team coaching, coaches, Hodge and Clutterbuck (2019) suggest, may benefit from engaging in different forms of professional support, for example group therapy or action learning sets. Here again, it would appear that team coaching can learn from the more established practice of group psychotherapy, which places emphasis on therapists engaging in group experience as part of their CPD to 'learn at an emotional level what you may have only known previously intellectually' (Yalom and Leszcz, 2005, p 553). Yalom and Leszcz argue that such knowledge includes experiencing how important it is to be accepted by the group, what self-disclosure really entails, feelings of vulnerability and hostility, as well as the therapist's own preferred role in a group and their habitual countertransference responses. In addition, Yalom and Leszcz extol the benefits of practitioners participating in group peer supervision to demonstrate the value of this kind of consultation and support.

Supervision and The PiE Team Coaching Model®

Supervision is a theme which runs through the three phases of The PiE Team Coaching Model® – Preparation, Intervention and Evaluation.

Preparation: here the focus of supervision is reflecting on ethical dilemmas and boundaries, including individual coaching arrangements and the dynamics of working with a co-coach. There may also be some apprehension about starting the work to reflect upon, especially as coaches usually comment that team coaching is more mentally and physically demanding than individual coaching.

Intervention: here the focus is on understanding how the work is impacting on the team coach, including triggers, transference and countertransference, and feelings towards team members. Supervision also provides a container for the team coach to download, an emotional space to replenish energy and the opportunity to stand back and refresh their approach to the work.

Evaluation: here the focus is on exploring endings – stepping out, leaving the leader and the team resourced for the future – and any hangover from the work, including what the team coach is taking away, and feelings and emotions associated with the assignment. In addition, this final space is a time to reflect on the quality of the work.

The evidence suggests that the practice of supervision will be an increasingly important element of team coaching in the future, focusing not just on the Evaluation phase, but also on the support the team coach needs from the initiation to the conclusion of an assignment. The Association of Coaching Supervisors and the European Mentoring and Coaching Council have both taken an interest in developing good practice and standards for team coaching supervision and establishing a body of knowledge about the differences between this and individual coach supervision, and this work is likely to gather pace. Team coaches are more and more likely to recognise the importance of undergoing supervision with someone who has the right experience to support this work, including an understanding of the dynamic complexity of groups and how the coach's own background and needs may influence their team coaching. Establishing supervision arrangements with the right supervisor is, therefore, an important consideration prior to team coaching commencing.

My experience of team coaching...

Holding

Challenger, supporter

On the edge

Buzzing, tired

Responsibility

— Gill

Conclusion

My motivation in writing this book was to produce a handbook for current and aspiring team coaching practitioners. A core theme running throughout the handbook is that there is no best or model way of team coaching, and my intention has been to describe the process and activities undertaken through the experiences and words of practising team coaches. In doing so, I set out to highlight some of the key questions team coaches need to address prior to commencing an assignment, some of the ethical issues to consider, as well as provide insight into activities undertaken under the umbrella of team coaching.

During the course of the handbook, we have reviewed how there is some universality of experience relating to elements of team coaching that are present in all types, genres and approaches to this type of coaching (Clutterbuck and Graves, 2023):

- It is a process that takes place over a number of sessions, spread out over a period of time.

- It involves individuals in a team learning together while completing a task/carrying out their business.

- It is holistic, focusing on the whole team.

- It involves work that necessitates the use of a coach (ie it is not simply team building).

- It focuses on the health of the team and long-term change.

However, there is significant divergence in theoretical/philosophical perspectives, personality preferences and developmental aspects among team coaches, resulting in different approaches in how this coaching is delivered. Team coaching is not a homogeneous practice; coaches develop their own approach, choosing what they perceive to be useful, and mixing and matching from the array of options on offer. As a result, there are many different forms of team coaching. While this may challenge any desire on the part of the coaching profession to have a neat conceptualisation of team coaching, it does provide plenty of choice for practitioners.

Coaches generally journey into team coaching via individual coaching, often having spent many years in one-to-one coaching. The disciplines of individual and team coaching have some similarities, but they also have some clear differences. As a practitioner, one of the fundamental differences between the two is that team coaching has distinct Preparation, Intervention and Evaluation phases with particular importance, time and attention given to the Preparation phase.

The Preparation phase has a dual purpose: providing insight for the assignment as well as opportunity for the team coach to create a safe environment, the latter being essential for the success of a team coaching intervention. This phase is also the time when the team coach needs to address some of the key questions relating to how they are going to structure and deliver the assignment, including whether they are going to work with a co-coach, coach the leader, coach other team members and provide the team leader with extra care and attention throughout the assignment. As we saw in Chapter Two, there are no clear-cut answers to these questions, but the chapter did highlight some of the ethical and practical issues for the team coach to consider.

The coaching literature and anecdotal feedback from team coaches illustrate that the role of team coach is a complex one. Of course, it necessitates the effective use of coaching skills, but also the ability to perform and move in and out of other roles, including those of facilitator, mentor and trainer. It is important that team coaches recognise why they are moving into a particular role, for example to share a model that they believe provides relevant insight for the team at that point in time, but it is also important that they recognise when they are becoming too comfortable and overplaying another role.

In addition to the roles that the team coach may consciously adopt, there are a number of roles that they may be inadvertently drawn into, including those relating to group contagion and those stemming from transference and countertransference. Insight into these roles is in its infancy and coaches are often only aware of being drawn into them in hindsight. This highlights the importance of team coaches making use of reflective practice and supervision from the initiation to the conclusion of an assignment.

A significant consideration for practitioners wanting to extend their individual coaching into team coaching is that coaches experience the latter as more challenging than the former and undergo more extreme emotions: the highs are higher and the lows are lower. The complexities of team coaching suggest that coaches practising this have greater need of supervision than individual coaches. Recent commentary acknowledges the physical and mental complexity and demands of team coaching for the practitioner (Hodge and Clutterbuck, 2019; Jacox, 2019; Lawrence, 2019; Thornton, 2019a; Thornton, 2019b; Graves, 2021).

There is increasing recognition of the importance of working with a supervisor who understands the complexity of groups, how the team coach's own background, family and professional, may influence their coaching, and that insight and learning can be gained from the practice of group psychotherapy, particularly for those practising co-coaching. However, the nature of supervision provided and how this is accessed by team coaches is highly variable. The Association of Coaching Supervisors and the European Mentoring and Coaching Council have both taken an interest in developing good practice and standards for team coach supervision, and in establishing a body of knowledge about the differences between one-to-one and team coach supervision, and we can expect that additional guidelines and frameworks will be published in the near future.

Evaluating the impact of team coaching remains problematic. As we have explored in this handbook, team coaching is a lengthy intervention, particularly if all aspects of the process are included: gathering insight from team members and stakeholders; working with a co-coach; carrying out multiple sessions; and possibly including individual coaching sessions for team members. The stakes are, therefore, high to demonstrate that it works, but current evaluation processes are often described as 'embryonic' or 'anecdotal', and tend to involve rerunning surveys and questionnaires used at the start of an assignment to demonstrate progress, feedback from team members and the intuition of team coaches based on specific moments or 'shifts' during sessions. As team coaching matures as a practice, it is likely that more robust methods of evaluation will be required. This is something for team coaches to bear in mind as they prepare for assignments.

Throughout this handbook, team coaching has been seen variously as a process that can be demanding and complex, but also hugely rewarding. While it may be somewhat frustrating that there is no one definition of team coaching or best way of delivering it, this also opens up a wealth of opportunity for the coach to create their own brand of team coaching based on their professional background, theoretical/philosophical perspective, CPD and personal preferences. There really is no one size fits all.

With this in mind, I concluded my study (Graves, 2021) with the development of The PiE Team Coaching Model® and accompanying framework, which represent the three key stages of team coaching: Preparation, Intervention and Evaluation. While I was initially reluctant to contribute another model to the growing number of team coaching models on the market, I believe that The PiE Team Coaching Model® and accompanying framework are different, having been developed through a collaborative research process in conjunction with other practising team coaches. They reflect the complexity of team coaching interventions by encapsulating the messiness of the theory in use and including both the essential universal elements as well as typical variations identified by team coaches.

The PiE Team Coaching Model® recognises the universal elements of team coaching as well as the fact that there are many divergences in practice. The supporting framework for the model (presented in Appendix A) provides a supplementary resource for the coaching profession, detailing universal elements as well as typical variations for team coaches to consider in their practice. The framework also provides a number of prompt questions, considerations and areas to reflect upon at each stage, enabling coaches to use this as an aid throughout a team coaching assignment.

I hope that you find the model and framework useful resources as you develop your practice as a team coach, and I would love to receive your feedback. Please do contact me on email via gill@iridiumconsulting.co.uk.

Appendix A
PiE Team Coaching Model®: Supporting Framework

Preparation phase

Questions to ask and answer

	'Typical' approaches	Variations
Do I need a co-coach? If so, who and how will we work together?	• For teams of eight or above, the coach will work with a co-coach, providing different personalities, experiences, insights; someone different for the participants to connect with and four eyes are better than two. Used to create shifts in energy. Banter with the co-coach can be used productively. Parallel process – a team working with another team.	• It's part of the contract: there will be two coaches. One may be lead coach. • For teams of up to eight to ten members, one coach will run the team coaching on their own, but it's a challenge to hold the numbers, as there's too much going on. It's physically and mentally demanding. • Only one coach is the team coach's preference, the philosophy being that working with another team coach would shift the dynamic in the room.
Do I coach the team leader? (Ethical and boundary issues. Transparency.)	• The team coach coaches the team leader.	• It's part of the contract: the team coach must coach the team leader. • The team leader has a separate coach with no involvement in the team coaching process. • The team coach's point of view is emergent; they will consider coaching the team leader if asked.

What special care does the team leader need? (Ethical and boundary issues. Transparency.)	• The team coach meets with the team leader first before engaging with the rest of the team, contracting with the leader, having a structured conversation on current team performance, stakeholders and outcomes.	• The team coach may or may not be coaching the team leader outside of the team coaching sessions. • Briefing sessions prior to or post team coaching interventions. • Sharing of data, eg output from team performance diagnostics/stakeholder interviews, prior to sharing with the whole team.
Do I coach other team members? (Ethical, boundary and capacity considerations. Transparency – who is working with whom? What will/will not be shared? Capacity – how many people can I coach at once?)	• No consistent approach.	• Everyone in the team has a coach. Two team coaches split the team members between them, with a supervisor for the two of them. • Individual coaching is offered to all team members at the outset, but everyone needs to be happy with any one-to-one relationship. • The team coach will only coach the team leader. • The team coach will coach team members who request coaching. This involves the challenge of managing boundaries/knowing too much.

(Continued)

Questions to ask and answer (cont.)

	'Typical' approaches	Variations
How will I gather insight for the assignment from team members?	• The team coach interviews all team members – what's working? What isn't working? What does 'good' look like? • Use of a team diagnostic (eg the TDS; Team Accelerator Model; TCI Team Diagnostic™). • This is the start of building individual relationships with the team members, creating trust and credibility.	• Use of a limited number of open-ended questions. • This is part of the contract: the coach would not embark on a piece of work without doing this. • Face-to-face or over-the-phone sessions.
How will I gather insight for the assignment from stakeholders?	• The team coach gains information from stakeholders regarding the performance of the team.	• Use of the Team Accelerator Model to get feedback from the team's commissioner and the stakeholders. • Stakeholder interviews. The team members are asked the same questions (eg five questions) and the answers are collated to feed back to the team.

		• Focus groups on site lasting up to a day for the next level down, perhaps the level below that and the level above. Where possible, customers will be interviewed too. The same questions are used consistently. • Data from 360 feedbacks.
What is the ideal length of the assignment?	• No consistent approach. Contracting tends to be about the number of sessions rather than the length of the assignment.	• No fixed timescale. The team coach will work with the team as long as is productive. A contract may be for a defined period of time, eg one year, with four to six meetings in this year, and then review. • Assignments are twelve to eighteen months. • Assignments are six to nine months.
What size should the team be?	• Five to twelve members, with eight usually being the maximum size for a team coach working on their own. Up to twelve with a co-coach.	
How many sessions?	• Typically four to six sessions.	• Longer assignments can be up to twelve sessions.

(Continued)

Questions to ask and answer (cont.)

	'Typical' approaches	Variations
How regular are the sessions?	• No consistent approach.	• Spacing of sessions varies from monthly, to every two months, quarterly or twice yearly. • With dispersed teams, there may be some meetings via phone or video in between face-to-face sessions.
How long are the sessions?	• Typically half-day sessions. • May start with lunch for ice breaking, followed by a session of around three-and-a-half hours.	• One full-day kick off followed by shorter half-day sessions. • One- to two-day kick off, then at least one half-to one-day follow-up three months later. • Full-day sessions. The morning is a normal team meeting with the team coach observing or facilitating. The afternoon is team coaching.

| A planned or fluid approach? | • The first session is generally planned, eg contracting – how are we going to work together? – and going through the output from the team diagnostic and team member and stakeholder feedback. The data is shared with the team and they decide what they want to work on.
• Use of a standard tool, eg Myers-Briggs, to provide a common language and understanding for all team members. | • Adopting a light-touch approach with psychometrics, although there's a belief that they can be a distraction and get in the way of what is happening in the room. Team coaches typically only use these at the client's request. Start with the work in hand and agree the agenda for the day.
• The team coach has a rough agenda or some ideas in their back pocket, but they work with what is current on the day.
• There's an overarching plan for the assignment and each session (eg first session: use of psychometric; second session: team purpose and charter). |

(Continued)

Questions to ask and answer (cont.)

	'Typical' approaches	Variations

Which tools and techniques should I use?	• A wide range of tools and techniques are used. The most popular are:
	
	  ○ Jungian type: the Myers-Briggs Type Indicator™ (MBTI), Insights Discovery™ or DISC™
	
	  ○ Strengths questionnaires (eg Strengthscope, StrengthsFinder)
	
	  ○ Eliciting team purpose, team charter and values
	
	  ○ Lencioni's Five Dysfunctions of a Team
		• Other tools and techniques used are:
		
		  ○ Team Accelerator Model
		  ○ TCI Team Diagnostic™
		  ○ TDS
		  ○ Team surveys (designed by team coach, pulled from various sources)
		  ○ The Rocket Model™
		  ○ Tuckman – theory of developmental sequences in small groups
		  ○ Leadership Climate Indicator
		  ○ The Hogan Team Report
		  ○ Neurolinguistic Programming (NLP)
		  ○ EBW Global Emotional Intelligence
		  ○ Clean language methodology
		  ○ Support and Challenge Model
		  ○ Change curve
		  ○ Gestalt chair exercises
		  ○ Systemic constellations
		  ○ Embodiment exercises, eg using Gottman's Four Horsemen
		  ○ Mindfulness and principles of meditation

Considerations for supervision

- Establishing a supervisory arrangement for the coach themselves and any co-coach

- Ethics and boundaries

- Issues of self-deception (how am I explaining taking on this work to myself?)

- Contracting

- Apprehension about starting the work

Intervention phase

Questions to ask and answer

	'Typical' approaches	Variations
How will I create a space for safety and growth? Some key considerations: • Credibility • Trust • Vulnerability • Psychological safety • Transparency	• The team coach clearly explains the process – how it works, the boundaries, confidentiality – consciously projecting the message, 'I know what I'm doing'. • They are aware of how to show up – being authentic. 'This is who I am'; 'I'm grounded, confident'; 'I've got this.' • The coach is listening to what is being said, but also to what is *not* being said. They're curious and inspire curiosity in the team. • They hold as much of a neutral 'adult' space as possible. 'I'm OK, you're OK.' • They role model dialogue and communication – asking questions, observing and noticing.	• Use of mindfulness practices for the coach to ground themselves and be present. • They deliberately use humour, eg to role model vulnerability and to let the team members know it's OK to get things wrong. • They use humour to make a connection (ensuring all participants are laughing at the same thing, but not at the expense of anyone) or to break down any 'us and them' feeling. • They role model behaviour to normalise it, eg saying, 'I'm confused'; 'I'm puzzled'; 'I don't know'. • They and their co-coach form a 'mini team' to role model effective dialogue and communication.

How will I challenge the performance of the team? Some key considerations:

- My preferences around challenge
- Being provocative
- Observational feedback
- Holding up the mirror

- Contracting around how challenge will be provided – by the team coaches and between team members, role modelling challenge and the team coach encouraging team members to challenge each other.
- Recognising and calling out behaviours, especially around living out team values and integrity, eg 'How does that fit with x?'
- Bringing into the here and now and raising awareness of what team members are experiencing and how this is impacting on them and others.
- Listening out for words, emotions and themes, going beyond the 'story' and playing back observations to the team.

- The kind of challenge depends on the personal comfort level and coaching philosophy of the coach, as well as the level of trust they've built with the team, often determined by how long they have worked with the team.
- Some team coaches regard themselves as being deliberately provocative and strong challengers.
- The coach uses themselves as a barometer for what is going on in the room and feeds this back to the team, eg 'I'm bored right now, is anyone else feeling this?'
- Offering a metaphor to team members based on what the coach is thinking or feeling and seeing if it resonates.

(Continued)

Questions to ask and answer (cont.)

'Typical' approaches	*Variations*
• Being present, noticing a pattern and if it keeps recurring. Sensing when to just hold this in their awareness or when to share this with the team. • Role modelling giving observational feedback. Pressing the pause button – 'What are you observing right now?'; 'What have you noticed?'; 'What is happening in the room?'; 'What isn't being said?' Providing an opportunity for team members to reflect. • Holding the space – being aware of attempts to avoid issues, to go off at a tangent – constantly returning to the team purpose and stakeholder requirements.	• Holding the space to model and reflect on fun and energy, eg 'How are we doing?'; 'How are you feeling?'; 'What's happening in the room right now with the energy?' • Working with their own intuition – noticing what's going on and the use of courage to ask questions. • Allowing team members time to rant/vent, followed by a directive 'holding to account' approach – eg 'What as leaders can you do around that?'; 'What as leaders are you role modelling?'

What roles might I choose to adopt? Why, how and when?	Performed well	Overplayed
The mentor or expert	• The coach brings in outside knowledge, eg of industry trends or the wider strategic perspective for the team to accept, reject or keep. They share their knowledge to provide insight/perspective.	• The coach is talking too much, sharing too much of their own expertise with the team, giving their opinion. It's more about the coach than about the team. • It's a role that can be projected on to the team coach by the team.
The teacher or trainer	• The team coach transfers a lot of what they do as skills to the team, sometimes through demonstrating the process (eg listening, asking questions, observational feedback) and sometimes through explaining, eg sharing a model to explain what might be going on in the team.	• The coach is doing too much of the talking, over sharing models or theory. They are feeling the pressure to 'give value for money'.

(Continued)

What roles might I choose to adopt? Why, how and when?	Performed well	Overplayed
The facilitator	- The coach is facilitating the process, designing the day, the flow of the session, the room, seating; creating and holding some structure and the time.	- The coach is grabbing the markers and flip-charting the discussions, starting to drive the agenda, pumping their energy into the room, being too active, filling silences. - They are feeling uncomfortable, diverting attention elsewhere.
The referee	- The coach is managing the process, helping the team make proactive, deliberate choices about what they're doing in the moment rather than being so free-flowing that it just flows away. Pointing out when 'we're off the pitch', eg not living out values, or going off topic.	- If overplayed, the referee can become the marshal, being too directive with the team.

What roles might I be drawn into? Why, how and when?

	The 'pull'	Signs to recognise it's happening
The de-facto team leader	<ul><li>There's a vacuum. The team leader isn't doing the role or doesn't really know how to.</li><li>The team coach is thinking, 'It's a comfortable role for me'; 'I've run big teams in multi-million-pound organisations'; 'I'm very happy leading.'</li></ul>	<ul><li>Everyone is looking at the coach rather than each other.</li><li>The team leader is deferring to the team coach, asking questions like, 'What do you think we should do?'</li><li>The team coach is volunteering (or in danger of volunteering) to take on things that might be helpful to move a particular process forward.</li></ul>
A member of the team	<ul><li>The coach is thinking, 'They're nice people, working hard, doing their best. I've worked with them a long time, I feel comfortable sitting with them in a business context – because that's where I came from. I miss being part of such a team, a sense of belonging.'</li></ul>	<ul><li>The coach normalises behaviour that they would previously have called out. They have a sense of 'Oh, that's just X being X' or 'That's just the banter in this team'. They forgive some of the foibles that they see and don't address them.</li><li>The coach is stepping in with solutions or opinions too much. They're playing the ball rather than standing back and looking at the interaction of other people playing with the ball.</li></ul>

(Continued)

What roles might I be drawn into? Why, how and when? (cont.)

	The 'pull'	Signs to recognise it's happening
The critical parent	• The coach is spotting 'childish' behaviours in the team – members having separate conversations, forming cliques, talking over each other, lowering energy, not wanting to do things, wanting someone else to hold them to account.	• The coach notices they're feeling frustrated, getting irritated. • They're noticing unfairness, people not listening, imbalance, lack of consideration for others. The coach is feeling that they're alone in calling these behaviours out, thinking, 'I can't be the only one noticing this is happening.'
The nurturing parent	• The coach wants to help the team members, sort them out, make things better for them. They're feeling sorry for team members who seem to be struggling.	• Being overly supportive of the team members: 'It really is tough for you guys'. Not challenging them in terms of how they step up. • Being drawn into team members wanting the coach to take their side.

Considerations for supervision

- Understanding how the work is impacting on the team coach – triggers, projection, countertransference and feelings towards team members.

- Awareness and understanding of how the team coach's own background and needs, family and professional, are manifesting themselves in their team coaching.

- Creating a container to download.

- Creating emotional space to replenish energy.

- Taking a standing-back and refreshing approach.

Evaluation phase

Questions to ask and answer

	Considerations
How am I developing my reflective practice as a team coach?	• Was this assignment team coaching or something else? What was asked for? What did I deliver? • What am I noticing about the development of my team coaching practice? • How does my one-to-one coaching inform my team coaching? Do I see myself as a better/stronger/different individual or team coach? What is my 'evidence'?
How am I evaluating the success of my team coaching?	• Rerunning surveys and seeing if scores improve or doing a 'pulse take', just looking at a few aspects the team has been working on. • Collecting anecdotal feedback from team members. • Noticing a shift and seeing some traction. Team members are proactively coming up with ideas about what they should do; I as the team coach am taking a back seat as the team is running itself. • Noticing the quality of conversations – team members having open conversations, challenging each other in a respectful way, saying how things are, sharing experiences, listening to each other, connecting with each other. There's a sense of productive rather than 'pretend' conversations. • Team members are able to be vulnerable with each other, challenge each other more. The 'undiscussables' are being discussed.

	- Stronger connections are being built stronger, with more wires on them.
- I'm observing a shift in the team leader, seeing them really standing up and challenging their team, noticing a shift in their authority – towards me as the team coach, and the team.
- Feedback from team members is that they are managing their processes better as a team and have more clarity around roles and boundaries.
- Feedback from stakeholders is positive.
- There's energy in the room. Team members leave on a high, although the proof of the pudding is later on. Do they follow through on their actions?
- Progress is not linear. It may be slow then fast, backwards, forwards or static. Assessing overall progress is hard as a team coach and may be a rollercoaster – exciting and scary.
How am I taking care of myself, tapping into external support and refreshing my energy levels?	- Self-care is important. Holding a team of six or more people is physically and mentally demanding, far more so than individual coaching. Recognise and allow for this when planning sessions, eg half rather than full days.
- Appreciate the importance of getting insight from all team members, as well as stakeholders where possible, to get as full a picture as you can prior to commencing the work.

(Continued)

Questions to ask and answer (cont.)

Considerations
• Appreciate the importance of having strategies for 'shaking off' the work, keeping some detachment from it.
• Appreciate the impact of where you sit – in the circle with the team or slightly detached.
• Engage in reflective practice with your co-coach to draw out learning.
• Engage in CPD to understand your own typical patterns, reactions and needs in a group setting.

Considerations for supervision

- Endings

- Stepping out, leaving the team resourced

- Processing any 'hangover' from the work

- Space to reflect on the quality of the work

- Engaging in supervision with a co-coach to explore parallel processes, transference, countertransference and themes emerging from the work

Appendix B
Team Effectiveness Survey Example

Below is a list of actions/behaviours that affect team performance. To what extent are these currently evident in your team? Please answer the eight questions using a scale of 1 (low) to 10 (high). Feel free to add any supporting comments or specific examples.

In addition, please provide your comments in response to the four open-ended questions at the end. Please answer the questions quickly and intuitively.

Return your completed questionnaire to ......

Rate and comment on these activities/behaviours in your team:

1. The team has a well-defined purpose and sense of identity   _ /10

   Comments/examples: ....

   ....

2. Team members know each other well and have a good sense of what makes each other 'tick'   _ /10

   Comments/examples: ....

   ....

3. The team is willing to surface issues and deal constructively with conflicts that arise   _ /10

   Comments/examples: ....

   ....

4. The team operates in a way that builds trust among its members   _ /10

   Comments/examples: ....

   ....

5. The team has a shared vision with clear, integrated goals   _ /10

   Comments/examples: ....

   ....

6. Team members tend to focus on constructive goals rather than on defending their positions   _ /**10**

   Comments/examples:..

   ....

7. The team is effective in eliciting the ideas and utilising the resources of all its members   _ /**10**

   Comments/examples:..

8. The team stays focused on the task at hand and reflects on process   _ /**10**

   Comments/examples:..

Please provide your views in answer to these four questions:

1. What top five adjectives would you use to describe this team?

2. Thinking about this team and how members work together, what would you most like to see change?

3. What sort of image would you say the team members collectively present?

4. If you could offer one piece of critical advice to this team, what would it be?

Appendix C
Psychometrics And Models Referenced

Books/articles

Blog Authors (2017) *Gestalt Therapy: The empty chair technique* (MentalHelp.net) www.mentalhelp.net/blogs/gestalt-therapy-the-empty-chair-technique, accessed 6 November 2023

Briggs Myers, I; Myers, PB (1995) *Gifts Differing: Understanding personality type – The original book behind the Myers-Briggs Type Indicator (MBTI) test* (Palo Alto, California: Davies-Black Publishing)

Curphy, G; Hogan, R (2012) *The Rocket Model: Practical advice for building high performing teams* (Tulsa: Hogan Press)

Kegan, R; Lahey, LL (2009) *Immunity to Change: How to overcome it and unlock the potential in yourself and your organization* (HBR Press)

Lawley, J; Tompkins, P (2000) (Clean Language Methodology) *Metaphors in Mind: Transformation through symbolic modelling* (Developing Company Press)

Lencioni, P (2002) *The Five Dysfunctions of a Team* (San Francisco: Jossey Bass)

Lisitsa, E (no date) *The Four Horsemen: Criticism, contempt, defensiveness, and stonewalling* (The Gottman Institute) www.gottman.com, accessed 3 November 2023

Price, C; Toye, S (2016) (The Team Accelerator Model) *How Organisations can Mobilize, Execute and Transform with Agility* (Oxford: John Wiley)

Prochaska, J; DiClemente, C (2005) 'The transtheoretical approach', in Norcross, JC; Goldfried, MR (editors) *Handbook of Psychotherapy Integration* (Oxford series in clinical psychology) (Second edition) (pp 147–171) (Oxford; New York: Oxford University Press)

Rath, T (2007) *StrengthsFinder 2.0* (Gallup)

Sandah, P; Phillips, A (2019) (TCI Team Diagnostic™) *Teams Unleashed* (London: John Murray Press)

Tuckman, BW (1965) 'Developmental sequences in small groups' *Psychological Bulletin* 63(6), 384–99, https://psycnet.apa.org/record/1965-12187-001, accessed 2 November 2023

Wageman, R; Hackman, JR; Lehman, E (2005) 'Diagnostic survey: Development of an instrument' *Journal of Applied Behavioral Science,* 41, p 373, https://journals.sagepub.com/doi/10.1177/0021886305281984, accessed 2 November 2023

West, C (2020) *The Karpman Drama Triangle Explained: A guide for coaches, managers, trainers, therapists – and everybody else* (CWTK Publications)

Whittington, J (2016) *Systemic Coaching and Constellations: The principles, practices and application for individuals, teams and groups* (London: Kogan Page)

Resources/tools

DiSC: www.discprofile.com/what-is-disc

EBW Global: www.ebwonline.com

Elisabeth Kübler-Ross Foundation: www.ekrfoundation.org/5-stages-of-grief/change-curve

Hogan Team Report: www.hoganassessments.com/reports/teams-report

Insights Discovery™: www.insights.com/products/insights-discovery

Leadership Climate Indicator (TALOGY): www.psionline.com/en-gb/assessments/leadership-climate-indicator

Neurolinguistic Programming (NLP?): www.nlp.com/what-is-nlp

Strengthscope: www.strengthscope.com

Support and Challenge Model: www.theleadershipcoaches.co.uk/post/leading-with-support-and-challenge

Team Diagnostics Survey: https://6teamconditions.com/services/diagnostics

References

Ancona, D; Perkins, D (2022) 'Family ghosts in the executive suite', *Harvard Business Review*, January–February, https://hbr.org/2022/01/family-ghosts-in-the-executive-suite, accessed 27 October 2023

Bachkirova, T (2016) The Self of the Coach: Conceptualization, Issues, and Opportunities for Practitioner Development', *Consulting Psychology Journal: Practice and Research*, 68(2), 143–156

Bachkirova, T; Kauffman, C (2009) 'The blind men and the elephant: Using criteria of universality and uniqueness in evaluating our attempts to define coaching', *Coaching: An International Journal of Theory, Research and Practice*, 2(2), pp 95–105 www.tandfonline.

com/doi/full/10.1080/17521880903102381, accessed 27 October 2023

Berne, E (1959) 'Principles of transactional analysis', *Indian Journal of Psychiatry,* volume 1; republished in *IJP,* 38(3) (1996) pp 154–159, www.ncbi.nlm.nih.gov/pmc/articles/PMC2970834, accessed 6 November 2023

Bharuvaney, G; Wolff, S; Druskat, V (2019) 'Emotion and team performance: Team coaching mindsets and practices for team interventions'. In Clutterbuck, D; Gannon, J; Hayes, S; Iordanou, I; Lowe, K; MacKie, D (Eds) *The Practitioner's Handbook of Team Coaching* (pp 192–209) (Oxon: Routledge)

Blakey, J; Day, I (2012) *Challenging Coaching: Going beyond traditional coaching to face the FACTS* (London: Nicholas Brealey)

Brown, SW; Grant, AM (2010) 'From GROW to GROUP: Theoretical issues and a practical model for group coaching in organisations', *Coaching: An International Journal of Theory, Research and Practice,* 3(1) pp 30–45 https://doi.org/10.1080/17521880903559697, accessed 27 October 2023

Campone, F; Awal, D (2012) 'Life's thumbprint: The impact of significant life events on coaches and their coaching', *Coaching: An International Journal of Theory, Research and Practice,* 5(1), pp 22–36, www.

tandfonline.com/doi/abs/10.1080/17521882.2011.64
8334, accessed 27 October 2023

Carr, C; Peters, J (2011) 'The experience of team
coaching: A dual case study', *International Coaching
Psychology Review*, 8(1), pp 80–98, https://explore.
bps.org.uk/content/bpsicpr/8/1/80, accessed 27
October 2023

Clutterbuck, D (2007) *Coaching the Team at Work*
(London: Good News Press)

Clutterbuck, D (2008) 'Coaching the team'. In Drake,
DB; Brennan, D; Gortz, K (Eds) *The Philosophy and
Practice of Coaching: Insights and issues for a new era*
(pp 219–238) (London: Wiley)

Clutterbuck, D (2014) 'Team coaching'. In Cox,
E; Bachkirova, T; Clutterbuck, D (Eds) (2014)
The Complete Handbook of Coaching (pp 271–283)
(London: Sage)

Clutterbuck, D; Gannon, J; Hayes, S; Iordanou, I;
Lowe, K; MacKie, D (Eds) (2019) *The Practitioner's
Handbook of Team Coaching* (pp 75–88) (Oxon:
Routledge)

Clutterbuck, D; Graves, G (2023) 'Team coaching'.
In Cox, E; Bachkirova, T; Clutterbuck, D (Eds) (2023)
The Complete Handbook of Coaching (pp 281–299)
(London: Sage)

Clutterbuck, D; Hodge, A (2019) 'Guidelines for team coaching supervision'. In Birch, J; Welch, P (Eds) *Coaching Supervision: Advancing practice, changing landscapes* (Routledge, Abingdon)

Cox, E; Bachkirova, T; Clutterbuck, D (2023) *The Complete Handbook of Coaching* (Fourth edition) (London: Sage)

Dassen, M (2015) 'Drama techniques in team coaching', *International Journal of Evidence Based Coaching and Mentoring*, 13(1), pp 43–57, https://psycnet.apa.org/record/2015-06090-004, accessed 27 October 2023

Edmondson, A (1999) 'Psychological safety and learning behavior in work teams', *Administrative Science Quarterly*, 44, pp 350–383 www.jstor.org/stable/2666999?origin=JSTOR-pdf, accessed 23 October 2023

Grant, AM (2009) *Workplace, Executive and Life Coaching: An annotated bibliography from the behavioural science and business literature* (Sydney, Australia: University of Sydney) www.duncansutherland.com.au/images/stories/downloads/coaching_bibliography.pdf, accessed 27 October 2023

Graves, G (2021) 'What do the experiences of team coaches tell us about the essential elements of team coaching?' *International Journal of Evidence Based*

Coaching and Mentoring, S15, pp 229–245, https://
radar.brookes.ac.uk/radar/items/fe000ae4-258d-
4fed-8fcb-8d2d484295e1/1, accessed 1 November
2023

Hackman, J; Wageman, R (2005) 'A theory of team
coaching', *Academy of Management Review*, 30(2),
pp 269–87, https://journals.aom.org/doi/10.5465/
amr.2005.16387885, accessed 1 November 2023

Hawkins, P (2011) *Leadership Team Coaching:
Developing collective transformational leadership*
(Philadelphia: Kogan Page)

Hawkins, P (2014) *Leadership Team Coaching in
Practice: Developing high-performing teams* (London:
Kogan Page)

Hodge, A (2021) 'Supervising team coaching'. In
Bachkirova, T; Jackson, P; Clutterbuck, D *Coaching
and Mentoring Supervision: Theory and practice* (Second
edition) (London: Open University Press)

Hodge, A; Clutterbuck, D (2019) 'Supervising team
coaches: Working with complexity at a distance'.
In Clutterbuck, D; Gannon, J; Hayes, S; Iordanou, I;
Lowe, K; MacKie, D (Eds) *The Practitioner's Handbook
of Team Coaching* (pp 331–342) (Oxon: Routledge)

Jackson, P; Bachkirova, T (2019) 'The 3 Ps of
Supervision and Coaching: Philosophy, Purpose and

Process', in Turner, E; Palmer, S (Eds) *The Heart of Coaching Supervision: Working with Reflection and Self-Care* (London: Routledge)

Jacox, B (2019) 'What are the key qualities and skills of an effective team coach?' In Clutterbuck, D; Gannon, J; Hayes, S; Iordanou, I; Lowe, K; MacKie, D (Eds) *The Practitioner's Handbook of Team Coaching* (pp 89–120) (Oxon: Routledge)

Jones, R (2016) 'The family dynamics we grew up with shape how we work', *Harvard Business Review* (19 July 2016) https://hbr.org/2016/07/the-family-dynamics-we-grew-up-with-shape-how-we-work, accessed 1 November 2023

Katzenbach, JR; Smith, DK (1993) *'The discipline of teams'*, *Harvard Business Review* https://hbr.org/1993/03/the-discipline-of-teams-2, accessed 1 November 2023

Lane, D (2006) 'The Emergence of Supervision Models', Presentation at the Annual Conference of the Special Group in Coaching Psychology of the BPS (unpublished)

Lawrence, P (2019) 'Defining team coaching: A practitioner perspective'. In Clutterbuck, D; Gannon, J; Hayes, S; Iordanou, I; Lowe, K; MacKie, D (Eds) *The Practitioner's Handbook of Team Coaching* (pp 331–342) (Oxon: Routledge)

Lawrence, P et al (2019) 'A dialogic approach to coaching teams'. In Clutterbuck, D; Gannon, J; Hayes, S; Iordanou, I; Lowe, K; MacKie, D (Eds) *The Practitioner's Handbook of Team Coaching* (pp.331–342) (Oxon: Routledge)

Leary-Joyce, J; Lines, H (2018) *Systemic Team Coaching* (London, England: Academy of Executive Coaching)

Lencioni, P (2016) 'Five Dysfunctions of a Team OC', YouTube, https://youtu.be/wHpB1EBufFo?si=5f074 bvnxacTIqvh, accessed 22 November 2023

Lowe, K; MacKie, D (Eds) *The Practitioner's Handbook of Team Coaching* (pp 331–342) (Oxon: Routledge)

Maxwell, A; Bluckert, P (2023) 'The Gestalt approach to coaching'. In Cox, E; Bachkirova T; Clutterbuck, D (Eds) (2023) *The Complete Handbook of Coaching* (pp 81–93) (London: Sage)

Mortensen, M (2015) 'Boundary Multiplicity: Rethinking Teams and Boundedness in the Light of Today's Collaborative Environment', INSEAD Working Paper No. 2015/31/OBH

Myers, A (2016) 'Researching the coaching process'. In Bachkirova, T; Spence, G; Drake, D (Eds) *The SAGE Handbook of Coaching* (London: Sage)

O'Connor, S; Cavanagh, M (2016) 'Group and team coaching'. In Bachkirova, T; Spence, G; Drake, D (Eds) *The SAGE Handbook of Coaching* (London: Sage)

Peters, J (2019) 'High performance team coaching: An evidence-based system to enable team effectiveness'. In Clutterbuck, D; Gannon, J; Hayes, S; Iordanou, I;

Peters, J; Carr, C (2013) *High Performance Team Coaching: A comprehensive system for leaders and coaches* (Canada: Freisen Press)

Senge, P (1990) *The fifth discipline: The art and practice of the learning organisation* (London: Doubleday / Bantam)

Stacey, R (2012) *Tools and Techniques of Leadership and Management: Meeting the Challenge of Complexity* (London: Routledge)

Thornton, C (2010) *Group and Team Coaching: The essential guide* (New York: Routledge)

Thornton, C (2019a) 'Beyond the theory of everything: Group analysis, conversation and five questions to choose theory in action with teams'. In Clutterbuck, D; Gannon, J; Hayes, S; Iordanou, I; Lowe, K; MacKie, D (Eds) *The Practitioner's Handbook of Team Coaching* (pp 210–219) (Oxon: Routledge)

Thornton, C (2019b) 'The making of a team coach'. In Clutterbuck, D; Gannon, J; Hayes, S; Iordanou, I; Lowe, K; MacKie, D (Eds) *The Practitioner's Handbook of Team Coaching* (pp 331–342) (Oxon: Routledge)

Wageman, R; Nunes, D; Burruss, J; Hackman, J (2008) *Senior Leadership Teams: What it takes to make them great* (Boston: Harvard Business School Press)

Woodhead, V (2011) 'How does coaching help to support team working? A case study in the NHS' *International Journal of Evidence Based Coaching and Mentoring, Special Issue No 5*, pp 102–119 https://radar.brookes.ac.uk/radar/items/8bdb6a42-d030-408f-b9e2-dff8b878c83f/1, accessed 1 November 2023

Woudstra, G (2021) *Mastering the Art of Team Coaching: A comprehensive guide to unleashing the power, purpose and potential in any team* (London: Team Coaching Studio Press)

Yalom, I; Leszcz, M (2005) *Theory and Practice of Group Psychotherapy* (New York: Basic Books)

Acknowledgements

Undertaking my professional doctorate and subsequently writing *Team Coaching with Impact at Work* has involved a considerable investment of time and effort. I certainly could not have got this far without the support of others. As befits a book on teams I would like to acknowledge and thank my personal support teams.

Firstly, a special thank you to my academic supervisor, Tatiana Bachkirova, for her support, challenge, presence and inspiration throughout my doctoral studies as well as encouragement to 'pick up my pen' and write this book.

A big thank you to all the team coaches I have worked with during my research for being so generous with their time. Their shared experiences, energy and enthusiasm made our work together productive and fun.

Thanks also to Alison Hodge, my coaching supervisor, for her support, for role modelling curiosity and for sparking my interest in some of the emerging debates in team coaching supervision.

Finally, thank you to my 'inner sanctum' support team. To Cathy for all her assistance over many years. From transcribing interviews and focus groups to designing complex illustrations – her versatility knows no bounds! To Colin for the endless discussions and especially for having complete faith in my abilities.

The Author

 Gill Graves is an experienced and highly regarded executive coach, team coach, coach supervisor, facilitator and consultant in leadership and team development. She specialises in enabling individuals and organisations achieve their goals and realise their full potential. Prior to founding Iridium in 2000, Gill was HRD Director of a US high-tech company with responsibility for Europe and Asia. She has extensive hands-on international experience, gained within fast-growing, rapidly changing environments across a range of different cultures and organisations.

Gill has an MBA from Warwick University, is a fellow of the CIPD and is accredited to the highest level, Master Practitioner, with the EMCC. She has a Professional Doctorate in Coaching and Mentoring from Oxford Brookes University, with her research focusing on the emergent practice of team coaching. Gill is a regular speaker at meetings and conferences and is the author of two highly-acclaimed books: *Presenting Yourself With Impact at Work* and *Coaching With Impact at Work*. Gill has built an impressive and loyal client base including Judge Business School, Mercedes, Cambridge University, Vodafone and the NHS. Learn more and get in touch at:

⊕ www.iridiumconsulting.co.uk